JEWELS FROM HEAVEN

JEWELS FROM HEAVEN

GOD SPOKE. . .SOMETIMES I UNDERSTOOD

PATT SALMEIER

XULON PRESS

Xulon Press
2301 Lucien Way #415
Maitland, FL 32751
407.339.4217
www.xulonpress.com

Printed in the United States of America.
Edited by Xulon Press.

ISBN-13: 9781545621257

DEDICATION

To the Lord:

I give thanks for His direction and help, for communing with me, giving me dreams and revelations, and most of all for helping me to write this book.

To my husband, Milo:

I give thanks for encouraging me to write and fulfill what the Lord inspired me to do.

TABLE OF CONTENTS

JEWELS FROM HEAVEN

In a dream, in a vision of the night, when deep sleep comes on men, while they take their rest on their beds; Then he [God] makes his secrets clear to men, so that they are full of fear at what they see; In order that man may be turned from his evil works, and that pride may be taken away from him. (Job 33:15-17 BBE)

Early spring of 1975, I asked the Lord to tell me when our baby would be born. For the next three nights, I dreamed and heard seven and five while seeing a clock. I knew the clock was associated with the numbers. Throughout the next three nights, the numbers were eight and four. Right after 12 a.m. on July 25, I began having contractions. I looked at the clock and the seven and five stood out. I realized it was 7/25, today's date. I knew our baby would definitely be born today. I woke up my husband and we prepared to leave for the hospital.

On the way to the hospital, I told my husband about the three nights of dreaming seven and five and the three nights of eight and four. We both thought the eight and four might be the time the baby would arrive, but our understanding was lacking as the eight and four were not connected to the clock. Our baby was born at 4:57 p.m. and the doctor said, "You have a healthy eight-pound baby girl." The nurse took the baby and said, "I think she is 8 pounds 4 ounces." This made me chuckle. Yes, our baby girl weighed 8 pounds 4 ounces.

I believe the Lord gave me this dream because I asked. He desires to reveal and affirm how involved He is in our individual lives and how precisely He knows the facts of what is and what will be.

God spoke through dreams to many in the Bible such as Jacob, Joseph, Pharaoh, Gideon, Nebuchadnezzar, Joseph (Jacob's son), and Joseph (Mary's husband) to name a few. The Lord is still speaking to people through their dreams today because, "He is the same yesterday, today, and forever" (Hebrews 13:8 NKJV).

It is possible that God is speaking to you through some of your dreams. In the Bible, dreams were given to instruct, warn, and foretell. The Lord still uses dreams, visions, and His spoken and written Word to enlighten, encourage, challenge, and change us. Getting God's understanding of how to interpret our dreams will keep us on God's chosen path.

During one worship time, the Lord called His dreams, visions, and spoken words "Jewels of Wisdom from Heaven." My understanding of this is dreams and visions are precious because they can add wealth to our understanding and way of life. They are valuable because they have the ability to add wisdom to our knowledge.

God speaks to each person according to his or her way of life and thinking based on what they have experienced growing up.

For instance, one of my friends loves animals and tells me their actions and responses give us knowledge of their characteristics and how they will express themselves in different situations. At a prayer meeting, I saw a camel come right up into my face—nose to nose after another person prayed. I was shocked and wondered why a camel would do that. Later, I asked my friend why a camel would come face to face with a human. Her response was, "When that happens, they are angry and are ready to spit in your face." I realized the picture was concerning the individual who prayed after

WE HEAR GOD WITH OUR HEARTS NOT OUR EARS.

me. I asked the Lord how to pray for that individual and prayed accordingly.

I believe the Lord has called me to write this book to show how God desires everyone to hear His voice and respond by communing with Him. God speaks to everyone in ways they will be able to understand, if they will only seek His heart.

Chapter 1

Dreams: Dealing with the Devil

Submit yourselves, then, to God. Resist the devil, and he will flee from you. Come near to God and he will come near to you. (James 4:7-8a)

I grew up in a nominal Christian home and only attended Sunday school occasionally. Therefore, my understanding of needing a personal Savior was lacking. When I was six years old, Jesus came to me in a dream. He was dressed in a white flowing robe and was descending down a towering spiral staircase. I raised my hands and screamed at Him, "Do not come, I'm not ready yet." I had no idea what that meant. It was several years before the truth dawned on me that I was a sinner headed for hell and needed Jesus to be my Savior.

When I was fourteen, I attended our church's revival. The evangelist vividly described hell and man's condition without Christ. I was convicted and knew I was not right with God. However, my pride and fear of man kept me from going forward to accept Jesus that night. Some of my fear of man resulted from my second grade teacher who humiliated me with her words about my lack of reading ability. Unfortunately, from that time on I believed the lie that I could not read very well or very quickly. If I had to read aloud, I would even stumble over words I knew because fear ruled my heart. I would not voluntarily read out loud.

Consequently, that fear kept me from going forward at the revival service and resulted in twenty-four hours of sheer terror that I would die before I could go to the next service. The second night of the revival service, I went to the altar and by faith received Jesus as my Savior and Lord. I have never regretted making my choice for Jesus.

When I was getting ready for bed that night, the Spirit of the Lord said to me, "Read your Bible." Having the Lord as my Savior gave me the grace, ability, and desire to read the Bible. Although reading was hard for me, I

IT TOOK YEARS OF THE LORD EXPOSING MY INCORRECT CONCEPTS OF HIM, BUT NOW I AM SECURE IN HIM (SEE ISAIAH 60:17).

had developed excellent retention. God's Word became my guide and source for my choices, actions, and words.

I had come to the Lord out of fear, but God's mercy, forgiveness, and grace taught me to come to Him out of love. I was so afraid of displeasing Him, I was not able to fully rest in the security of His love, salvation, and peace until I embraced this truth.

Dealing with the Devil

God gives us dreams for many reasons. One reason is so we will learn what we need to know about our enemy, the devil.

Dream: My husband, Milo, got up early to go to a men's prayer breakfast and forgot to shut and lock the front door. When I get up, the door was wide open. I began looking through the rest of the house, but do not see any one. When I returned to shut the front door, a teenage girl ran from the kitchen. I caught her and yelled for my children to call the police. "What are you doing here?" I ask her as I held her tightly. She wiggled and squirmed trying to get away from me. Suddenly, she started holding her stomach and complaining of pain in her side. When I ask her what was wrong, she responded, "I have a tumor and the pain is so great that I don't know what I am doing."

Suddenly, our friends Alice and Wayne came in the door, called her by name, and asked her what she was doing in my house.

Then the scene changed. Milo and I were out walking and I just started praising the Lord in the Spirit. This same girl was following us and started to praise the Lord in tongues, too. Milo turned to me and said, "That's the way to lead people into praying in the Spirit." [End of dream]

A few days later, I decided to go to the Bible Book Store to visit with the owner. As I walked in the front door, the owner surprised me by saying, "I'm glad you're here. I've been waiting for you to come and pray for this woman." I see a woman holding her stomach and in great pain.

I went to the woman and began praying for her to be healed in Jesus' name. I commanded all demonic activity to cease and leave in Jesus' powerful name. The woman was instantly healed and the pain in her stomach was gone. I asked her if she wanted to accept Jesus and she said she did, so I led her in the prayer of salvation and repentance. Then I asked her if she wanted to receive the baptism of the Holy Spirit and again she said she did.

A few weeks later, the churches of the city gathered for a New Year's Eve party. The woman I had prayed for in the Christian Book Store was there. I started talking to her. She mentioned Wayne saying he was a customer of hers who had shared Jesus with her several times before I had prayed for her that day.

Then she began to tell me how she was to have been the third witch in a witches' triangle that was to be set up over the city. "You leading me to faith in Christ prevented that from happening," she said.

Not knowing what a witches' triangle was, I asked her to explain. "It is when three witches or warlocks strategically purchase property in a city where their properties create a triangle over the city for the purpose of oppressing those who live under the triangle." Interestingly, the motel she owned was at the edge of town. A witches' coven was in a second corner. I did not know where the third one lived.

All I could do was stand in awe of our mighty, loving, compassionate God for using me to help save, free, and protect His people from potential demonic oppression.

You can see by reading this true story how God gives dreams so we will learn what we need to know about our enemy, the devil and how great is the power and love of our God.

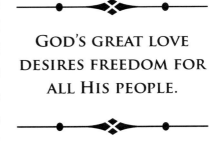

GOD'S GREAT LOVE DESIRES FREEDOM FOR ALL HIS PEOPLE.

The Lord showed me through this dream:

- He was sending someone He wanted me to lead through deliverance from Satan.
- There would be a salvation and a baptism in the Holy Spirit.

- The woman and I would have a common acquaintance.
- God protects His people.

After this, my friend Caren and I ministered to one of her acquaintances, she told us she too had been a witch. I could hardly believe all she told us about the work of Satan using witches to do his bidding. She told us the horrendous things she had done as a witch. Once she even translated herself to her enemy's bedroom while He was sleeping in order to murder him, though she left without killing him.

"I want you to know that Christians do not have the unity that witches have, consequently, they do not have the power we have," she told us. "Only when Christians come into unity will they be able to overpower the enemy and his workers."

Hearing this caused us to do heavy spiritual warfare that day. We then began to teach unity of Christians is essential to confronting and pulling down the forces of evil.

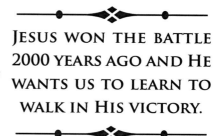

JESUS WON THE BATTLE 2000 YEARS AGO AND HE WANTS US TO LEARN TO WALK IN HIS VICTORY.

In a more recent dream, I was looking up into the sky seeing a regiment of twin dots that appeared to be in military formation spread out from east to west, row after row.

A man to my right raised his arm, pointed to them and yelled, "Bombs." I looked right above me seeing a set of twin bombs falling towards me. I started praying in the Spirit and the bombs moved to the right of me unable to reach me. Then another set positioned itself over me, but as I prayed in the Spirit, they also moved to the right. As long as I prayed in the Spirit, the bombs were not allowed to fall on me. I awakened realizing the great power of praying in the Spirit.

I asked the Lord what He wanted me to learn from this dream. Through the next few weeks, He revealed the twin dots represent the one-two punch of Satan. Then the Lord showed me how Satan used this same one-two punch on Eve causing her to question His instructions to her. Satan's words caused her to doubt God's integrity and disobey Him. Satan is still using these same words to cause doubt throughout the world so mankind will fall under the power of his deception.

Most do not realize they have been deceived when they begin to question God's love, goodness, and forgiveness. The truth is God is good all the time. His Word can be trusted. In fact, Jesus used the Word of God to refute the devil in Matthew 4:1-11. His way should be our way of dealing with Satan and his ploys.

What should I do? I will pray with my spirit, but I will also pray with my mind. I will sing praises with my spirit, but I will also sing praises with my mind. (1 Corinthians 14:15 NET)

Besides salvation, praying in the Spirit has been one of the greatest assets in my Christian life. When I don't know how to pray, I pray in the Spirit. When I see harm coming my way, I pray in the Spirit. When I am startled or something unexpected happens, I just start praying in the Spirit without thinking about it. It is after praying in the Spirit that I receive most revelation and understanding.

Shortly before we left our second pastorate, I went to a Christian meeting with a couple of friends. They had a door prize and I won an atlas. I had an inner "knowing" our family would be moving. A few weeks later, I dreamed we were given a promotion and our salary would be increased. It wasn't very long before we were invited to try out as pastors for a larger church with a larger salary. We went for an interview and they wanted us to come immediately. A few weeks later, we were in a new parsonage in another state. It was in this place I learned a lot more about dreams, spiritual warfare, and what God needed to change in me so I could grow and fulfill the mission He had given me.

A few months later, I dreamed a mother wanted me to work with her demonically oppressed son, so he would be delivered from the enemy's hand. When he came, I dealt with the demon called, "Slovak Activities." It was an extremely strong spirit, but I finally obtained victory in Jesus' name.

The dream then changed scenes. I was in a car with my sister and "Slovak Activities" came in and started pushing me down. Its power caused my sister to pass out. I woke up frightened. I started praying in the spirit and fell back to sleep. Then I dreamed there was a man who was mocking me for casting out demons. I prayed that God would open his eyes to see the spiritual forces at work. As he lifted his head, his face revealed that he was seeing the world of evil spirits. [End of dream.]

After moving to our new parsonage, I learned the people in the town were predominately from Slovak countries. This gave me understanding as to why the spirit was called "Slovak Activities." The people of this area were demonically oppressed. I was harassed there because I was not yet aware of the open doors I had of fear, rejection, and doubting God's integrity.

I knew God had given me power and authority over the enemy, but my fear opened wide the door for Satan's harassment. His foothold in my life was totally exposed while we lived in that town. It was truly a training ground for me to learn more about God's love and power in my life. While there, many people's eyes were opened to the spiritual world and the knowledge of Ephesians 6:12-13.

> *For our struggle is not against flesh and blood, but against the rulers, against the authorities, against the powers of this dark world and against the spiritual forces of evil in the heavenly realms. Therefore put on the full armor of God, so that when the day of evil comes, you may be able to stand your ground, and after you have done everything, to stand.*

In the late 70s, a woman I knew wanted to be free from demonic harassment, oppression, and all that goes with it. I led her through deliverance. That night I dreamed that I kept hearing her call the demons back. I could see them as black mists around her. [End of dream.]

The next day I called this woman and told her what the Lord had shown me in this dream. She said, "Yes, I did call them back. I was lonely and I wanted to know where they went."

I said, "As a Christian, this is a wrong thing to do. You must decide either to be free through the power of Jesus or live under demons and their harassment for the rest of your life."

She decided she wanted freedom in Christ. I led her through deliverance again. After that she stayed free from demonic oppression.

Another time, I dreamed my mother called to tell me that she would be sending Jimmy Carter to our church for deliverance. When Jimmy Carter arrived, he brought a peanut butter and pickle sandwich. Upon awakening, I figured this must represent someone important was coming to our church. Surely, the President of the United States would not come to our house or church. I pondered that dream for about two years, but finally put the dream aside.

Then one Sunday morning, Milo was about ready to ask for testimonies from the people when the church door opened. In came a young man looking like he was stoned. He went to the front row and sat down.

When Milo asked for testimonies, the young man stood up and said, "I am Jimmy Carter, President of the United States of America, and I have very heavy responsibilities. Please pray for me."

I started singing, "Jesus, Jesus, Jesus there is something about that name...."[1]

The young man then stood up and walked out. The Lord spoke to my heart to go out and talk to him, but I argued with the Lord about approaching a crazy man. I felt great pressure from the Lord to go out, but I continued to resist.

Thinking he had probably left, I finally obeyed. I found the man sitting on the top step of the church stairs.

Gaining strength and courage from the Lord, I asked him one question, "Do you want to be free?"

He responded, "Yes."

I commanded, "Satan, loose him in the name of Jesus Christ."

The young man's arms flew up in the air and out of his mouth came this beautiful prayer language. I was surprised as this congregation did not hold to speaking in tongues. Now this oppressed man who had just been delivered from demons was praying quite loudly in his heavenly language. I asked him to come back in to the church and tell the people what God had done for him.

After the service, I asked his real name and why he'd said he was Jimmy Carter.

He said, "The demons inside of me told me to say that."

He then told me his real name and that he was a son of a Pentecostal preacher. He also said that he had just been released from prison the day before and the Lord had told him he was to be in our church the next morning or it would be his last chance to get right with Him. He arrived in town shortly after the Sunday service started.

I later learned he had been at our church years before, so he knew what church God was talking about. He also told me everything he had participated in that resulted in his going to prison. He knew he had not been pleasing the Lord.

He stayed with us three days. I was concerned for him because I knew he needed good Christian support and love. The night he left, the Lord gave me a dream revealing this man was leaving and spoke Jeremiah 1:12b to me. "I am watching over my word to perform it" (NASB). I knew He had started a work in this young man and would complete it (see Philippians 1:6) so I did not have to be concerned about him.

Many times in my dreams, I have found that my Mom represented the Holy Spirit as He is the one who guides, nurtures, and teaches us (see John 14). Therefore, in this dream, it was Holy Spirit who sent this "Jimmy Carter" to us. You may be wondering what the peanut butter and dill pickle sandwich means. It was because the Lord had previously given my husband and me our prayer languages according to 1 Corinthians 14:2-4. Since the church did not believe in tongues, those of us who embraced this power of praying in the spirit used the word peanut butter when speaking about tongues. If one speaks with peanut butter in his or her mouth, words are gabbled and are not understood. The dill pickle represents what is sour and often not tolerated by some, just as tongues or a prayer language is unacceptable to some people.

God used this to teach us how He has full knowledge of our vernacular and the meanings we give to words. The Lord was communicating in a way I would understand; although, it took a while to fully understand the whole dream. He was telling me to be looking for a "Jimmy Carter" not President Jimmy Carter. What an amazing God we serve!

HE EVEN KNOWS AND SPEAKS OUR PRIVATE LANGUAGE AND HE KNOWS WHAT WE WILL FINALLY UNDERSTAND.

Hearing God through Dreams and Visions

At the end of each chapter, I suggest you stop and review what God taught me through dreams and visions so you too can learn from my experiences. In this chapter, I learned the power of praying in the Spirit. It has been one of the greatest assets in my Christian life. When I don't know how to pray, I pray in the Spirit. When I see harm coming my way, I pray in the Spirit. When I am startled or something unexpected happens, I just start praying in the Spirit without thinking about it. It is after praying in the Spirit that I receive most revelation and understanding.

Ephesians 6:12-13 and 18 tells us:

- Our struggle is not against _____ and _____,

- But against the rulers, against the authorities, against the powers of this dark world and against the _____ _____ of _____ in the heavenly realms.

- Therefore, put on the full armor of God, so that when the day of evil comes, you may be able to _____ _____ _____.

- And after you have done everything, to _____.

- And pray in the _____ on all occasions with all kinds of prayers and requests.

- With this in mind, be _____ and always keep on _____ for all the saints.

Read Ephesians 6:14-17 and list the armor of God.

- The belt of _____. Where do you find this truth? _____

- The breastplate of _____ which means _____

- Your feet fitted with the gospel of _____. Who gives you this? _____

- The shield of _____ to extinguish _____. Where must you place your faith? _____

- The helmet of _____. Have you accepted Jesus Christ as your Lord and Savior? _____ (If not see the prayer below.)
- The sword of the _____ which is the _____ of God.

Pray: *Father God, I thank You for the dreams and visions You use to teach and equip me concerning spiritual warfare and dealing with the devil and his army. Thank You for the armor You have provided to achieve the victory Jesus has already won for me. I praise and worship You for Your great love and the power and authority You have given me to pray for and deliver others from the oppression of the enemy. In Jesus' name I pray.*

If you have never accepted Jesus as your Lord and Savior, simply pray: *Lord Jesus, thank You for dying on the cross that I might be forgiven for my sins. I repent today of my sins and ask You to forgive me and come into my heart and life, and lead me into victory in You. I believe You are the Son of God and have risen from the dead according to Romans 10:9. Please send Your Holy Spirit to baptize me with power according to* 1 Corinthians 14:2-4 *that I can more effectively do the spiritual warfare needed to pray for and deliver others from the enemy's oppression. In Jesus' name I pray.*

Chapter 2

DREAMS, VISIONS AND GOD BREATHED WORDS: HELPING OTHERS RUN THEIR RACES

Therefore, since we are surrounded by such a great cloud of witnesses, let us throw off everything that hinders and the sin that so easily entangles. And let us run with perseverance the race marked out for us, fixing our eyes on Jesus, the pioneer and perfecter of faith. For the joy set before him he endured the cross, scorning its shame, and sat down at the right hand of the throne of God. (Hebrews 12:1-2)

I heard the Lord say, "Though it seems like you are going nowhere, keep going. You must run the race before you, in order to finish the race I have given you."

No one who puts his hand to the plow and looks back is fit for service in the kingdom of God. (Luke 9:62)

While praying I had this vision: I was standing still on the ledge of a cliff. There was a red carpet runner under my feet. I looked down the runner to see where it was coming from and there was an individual climbing up it. I didn't offer my hand and he didn't ask for it. I decided I must be in the way and stepped off the runner. The first individual came up holding the hand of another. This repeated several times while I was watching.

I repented for being in the way, but the Lord impressed me that I was just an observer.

He said, "These are the ones I'm using to bring the lost to Me. They are a part of My pure bride. They willingly lend a hand to bring another into My kingdom."

We only lead others to the Lord by claiming the Blood of Jesus [the red carpet].

I saw the Lord carry me into the mire. From that position, I could see many, many people inundated with the mire. They were literally drowning.

I said, "O Lord, send what is needed to bring the lost to godly sorrow that brings forth repentance. Let mercy, truth, and righteousness permeate their lives until they recognize their need of You."

In 1977, I had a very short, pointed dream. I saw the Book of Life come before my eyes. I read the second paragraph on the left which said, "Your purpose is to clear the gates of souls." Then the book was taken back into heaven. I knew there were other words on the page, but I was not able to read them.

I understood this meant God would use me to help people get free from every weight and sin that would hinder their growth in Christ, so they would be able to run with endurance the race that the Lord set before them. They would find the importance of focusing and keeping their eyes on Jesus.

Years ago, I was reading the book *Something More* by Catherine Marshall. She had written about God speaking to us in dreams, so I told the Lord that I would like Him to speak to me in my dreams.

Shortly, after I dreamed: Amy, a friend of our daughter Susan, had come to the Children's Crusade we were having. During these services, Amy accepted the Lord as her Savior. She stood up from the altar and said, "Jesus is my All in All." [Even in the dream, I wonder why a second-grader was saying "Jesus is my All in All?" Does she even understand what that means?] In the dream, a couple of weeks after the crusade Amy died. The whole second grade class was upset by her death, so Amy's mother comes to the class to tell the children that everything is alright; "Amy is with God because Jesus is her All in All." [End of dream].

About three weeks later, I dreamed that my husband, children, and I were traveling on a lonely one-lane steep and curvy mountain road. The road had numerous switchbacks and was so narrow that any oncoming car would require one of the vehicles to pull off the road's shoulder. All of a sudden, in the distance, headlights appeared.

I woke up panicked, because we were headed for a head on collision.

Another three weeks passed and I had the same dream again only the cars were closer together this time. Again, I awoke panicked. Within another three weeks, I had the same dream a third time, only this time we were going around a curve and we hit head on. I woke up with my adrenalin running and saying within myself, *I refuse to ever have this dream again.* [I don't know how I could have stopped it, but that was my declaration.]

I do believe the Lord was gracious by giving me the three latter dreams. It helped me understand the former dream was foretelling an upcoming death. Maybe, if I had more understanding and discernment at that time, I could have interceded in prayer and seen a miracle. God had spoken, but I did not understand.

A few days after this last dream, I was walking down the street and saw Mr. P. His wife was a member of our church. I knew he never claimed to be a Christian. With my spiritual eyes I could see death was on him. I went home and asked my husband, who was the pastor of our church, to go see Mr. P. I just knew Mr. P. was going to die. While Milo was visiting him, Mr. P. accepted Jesus as his personal Savior.

Approximately a week later, Mrs. P. called to tell us that her husband was in the hospital, and would Milo please visit him. Milo was glad to do so. A few days later, Mrs. P. asked us to pick her husband up from the hospital as he was being released and she would be teaching.

As usual, the hospital was slow getting the needed papers together for his release, so we just sat and visited. Mr. P. realized I was pregnant and asked when our baby was due. I told him the middle of July. Mr. P. looked up at the ceiling as if seeing something in a distance. I knew he was thinking, "I won't see this baby." A few minutes later, the hospital released him. We took him home. Mrs. P. called a half hour later to tell us Mr. P. had passed away.

Milo left immediately to spend some time with the grieving family. I fell to my knees to pray. I had to know for sure Mr. P. really had made Jesus Lord.

The Lord responded to my cry with, "Patt, do you remember that dream about Amy?"

I said, "Yes, but why would you show me Mr. P. as a girl?"

The Lord answered, "Because he is My beloved child."

I later learned the name Amy means "beloved." Mr. P. was one of God's beloved children. All I could do was praise the Lord because Mr. P. was with his Lord and Savior.

> There is neither Jew nor Greek, slave nor
> free, male nor female, for you are all one in
> Christ Jesus." (Galatians 3:28 NIV)

This dream revealed even more as Mrs. P. was the second-grade teacher and her husband's death upset the whole second grade class. Mrs. P. assured her class everything was alright as Jesus was Mr. P.'s "All in All." God had spoken, but I hadn't understood. I realized all those dreams were foretelling Mr. P's death and that I could be assured that all was well with his soul. God hears our cries and directs our steps. He is not willing that any should perish.

Another time, I dreamed that a man in our church was remodeling his home for his wife, Jill. I was truly amazed as I walked through it upon completion. There wasn't any place in the house where a shadow could be found. Every room was so full of light. All I could do was stand in awe.

I knew from this dream that Jesus was Jill's husband and He was going to bring His light into every room of her life so there would be no shadows of darkness. I wasn't very discerning about what was really in Jill's life when pastoring there. Her life had revealed godly speech, she knew the truths about Jesus, and she served in the church. Her life appeared Christian.

However, a few years after we left, we had a chance to visit her. Her first words to us were, "I have to tell you the truth about my life. I was an alcoholic, but I kept it secret. No one knew. After you left, someone in the church saw me going into the liquor store and reported it to the pastor. The pastor called asking me to come in and talk to him. At the meeting, he told me what had been reported. I confessed the truth of my alcoholic condition. He removed me from the position I held in the church and it broke my heart."

Jill went on to say that the talk with the pastor sent her to Jesus. She saw she had grieved God's heart as well as the pastor's. She repented.

She then said, "I have not had a drink from that time."

Praise the Lord! He is so faithful to fulfill His spoken word. The Lord had definitely put light in all the rooms of her life. Then He allowed me to see the fulfillment of the dream. Thank you, Jesus.

In the late '70s, I dreamed that I was on an old dusty road. Tall old trees were growing along each side. At the end of the road was a plowed field ready to be seeded. I picked up seeds from the road, but they were shriveled. I went to the end of the road and found a box with excellent seed. I took them back to the plowed field. As I was planting the seeds, two of the seeds sprouted in my hand. I placed them in the ground and leaves immediately came forth.

This dream had to do with the people we pastored at that time. Some of them would not grow because they were shriveled in their spirits as a result of not responding to the Spirit of God or His Word. Others, like the good seed, were hungry for God and grew accordingly. As we ministered in that town, there were two main people who had phenomenal spiritual growth and are still growing in

Christ today. Others grew slightly and some not at all, just like the seeds in the dream.

I had another dream concerning a woman in this same church: I dreamed I had three gifts to give her. The gifts were a red scarf, a white baby dress, and a package of diaper pins. I went down into her basement where she was washing clothes. She had a tall stack of linens on the open door of her conventional washing machine. I tried to hide two of the three gifts behind my back so she wouldn't see them. Something happened causing the red scarf and the baby dress to be sucked into the motor of the washing machine. We pushed the machine over causing the linens to be soiled. We were both trying to pull them out. I then noticed the package of diapers pins was pinned to her wall out of normal vision range, as was what they represented.]

When I awoke, I thought, *How weird. Why would I do that and what did it mean?*

A few weeks went by and the Lord told me to go minister to this woman. I argued with the Lord saying, "I am the one who needs to be ministered to today, not to minister."

His response was, "I ministered when I was weak and weary."

I said, "Alright, Lord" and went to talk to her.

As a result of our conversation, I realized she needed a clean robe of righteousness [the white baby dress] as she was out of fellowship with the Lord. I ministered to her and she came to peace with God. I then encouraged her to stay faithful and follow Jesus wherever He leads.

The two gifts caught in the motor revealed her spiritual condition was caught up in works not faith. Therefore, her righteousness was not lining up with the Word of God.

As I was leaving her home, I remembered the dream and realized that I had just delivered the white baby dress. Then I wondered what the red flag meant. I instantly saw with my spiritual eyes a red flag hanging from the back of a truck [a warning of a load that is over extended].

I then knew the Lord was saying, "You just delivered My righteousness and my warning."

A few days later, as I was pondering what the diaper pins represented, I heard, "You are going to pin her down. Either she is going to serve me or she is not."

The thought of that frightened me. Everyone had told me the gift of exhortation is only to be used to lift others up. The thought of confronting someone was not desirable and could cause strife. However, I knew, "All Scripture is God-breathed and is useful for teaching, rebuking, [refuting error] correcting [to make right or to amend] and training in righteousness, so that the man of

God may be thoroughly equipped for every good work" (2 Timothy 3:16-17).

A few more weeks went by and I started having the anointing of God on me so strong that it felt like I had cobwebs tickling my forehead. I kept trying to rub it off.

The third day of this anointing was Sunday and in the service the Lord spoke to me and said, "This is the day and now is the time to pin her down."

The anointing and peace were so great I knew it was right and nothing would go wrong. So, after the service, I asked my husband to call and make an appointment for this woman and her husband [both were leaders in the Church] to come to a meeting in the afternoon. They agreed to come.

My husband said to me, "Patt, you had better be right."

The anointing of God was so great the only thing I could say was, "It will be alright."

They came and I begin to tell her what the Lord had said, "He wants to pin you down. Either you are going to serve the Lord or you're not."

She was furious and said, "Who do you think you are. Do you think you are God?"

I calmly told her, "I know I am not God. However, there is one thing I do know. God loves us so much that when we are not listening to Him, He will graciously send someone to bring His spoken word [rhema] to awaken us. He does not want anyone to go into destruction."

She replied, "I don't have to listen to this. I am going home."

Her husband could not believe she refused to deal with what was just presented.

They left and Milo said, "Patt, you just destroyed this church."

My response was, "Everything will be alright."

The next morning the anointing was gone and I said, "Oh no, I just destroyed this church."

I spent the next three days studying the Bible about exhorting, correcting, rebuking, etc. I was sure she wouldn't darken the door of the church again.

Wednesday night service came and she did not show up. After the service started, she came in, walked to where I was seated, and handed me a letter [which I still have today].

I thought, *Oh no, this is a resignation letter. I'm in big trouble.*

"First, I want to ask your forgiveness," she wrote. "My pride was at an all-time high. I knew you were speaking truth, but I did not want to hear or accept it. God had already been speaking to me—showing me what I looked like to Him. He showed me, 'my righteousness was as filthy rags.'" Then she said since she was so miserable, she decided to take some time away from family and home just to pray. While in prayer the Lord asked her a question from Isaiah, "*Why spend money on what is not bread, and your labor on what does not satisfy? Listen to me, and eat what is good, and your soul will delight in the richest of fare. Give ear and come to me; hear me, that your soul may live"* (Isaiah 55:2-3 NIV). She went on to say, "God is now driving and I am in the back seat of my life."

Three weeks later, her husband testified to the fact that his wife had changed so much that he was living with a new woman. They are still serving the Lord today. All praise to God and His faithfulness.

HOW GREAT IS GOD'S LOVE!

In the late 1990s, the Lord said, *"There is a veil of mourning coming to America."*

His word was fulfilled with Columbine, 9-11, and the terrorist attacks that have since followed. I believe America mourned for itself and not for her sin. I have prayed continually for America to recognize her sin and have godly sorrow that leads to repentance.

> *If My people who are called by My name will humble themselves, and pray and seek My face, and turn from their wicked ways, then*

I will hear from heaven, and I will forgive their sin and heal their land. (2 Chronicles 7:14 NKJV)

Helping Others Run Their Race

I can't even remember how many times I dreamed this particular dream: I was at Mom's house. It was filthy with cobwebs, dirt piled high, cluttered with piles of dirty laundry and stacks of dirty dishes to be washed. I would dig in and get the house all cleaned up, only to find it in the same condition the next time.

This was not true of my mother in the natural, so I knew Mom's house represented the church and the believers who clutter God's house with their flesh and unconfessed sin. No matter what counsel was given, it was to no avail. It takes the conviction of the Holy Spirit to bring one to repentance. They may have recognized their sin, but made no change in their lives. All I could do was pray for the Holy Spirit to move upon their hearts.

For those who live according to the flesh set their minds on the things of the flesh, but those who live according to the Spirit set their minds on the things of the Spirit.

To set the mind on the flesh is death, but to set the mind on the Spirit is life and peace. For the mind that is set on the flesh is hostile to God; it does not submit to God's law, indeed it cannot; and those who are in the flesh cannot please God. (Romans 8:5-8 RSV)

- **Does your heart and conscience need a cleansing? If so, Jesus is waiting for you to respond to Him.**

Pray: *Father God, I thank You for the dreams and visions that help me to run my race so I can then help others run their race as well. Thank You for hearing our cries and directing our steps. Thank You that You are not willing that any should perish. Show me how to better serve You and minister to those You have called to do Your kingdom work. In Jesus' name I pray.*

Chapter 3
Dreams: Used in the Prophetic

I n the early '90s, the Lord led me into my subconscious
mind. I could see a young woman who was skillfully
playing the piano. I understood I was that woman and
musical ability was locked up within me. I had believed
what my sister had spoken over me when she said, "You
have no musical ability and I will never go to church again,
if you ever open your mouth to sing."

In my subconscious mind, I saw a big door that was
locked. Jesus couldn't open it until I let Him. I chose to
do His will, so He took a key and unlocked it. All that was
behind the door was water. It poured out into all the rooms
of my subconscious mind.

The Lord said, "You have bottled up and not given out
the things you received in the Spirit to the point that you are

no longer receiving a fresh supply from Holy Spirit."

At that point, conviction and repentance hit me. I chose to let God's Spirit clean my subconscious mind and heal me. It was after this I started singing prophetically.

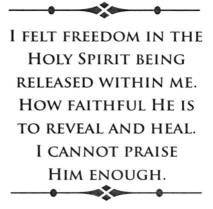

I FELT FREEDOM IN THE HOLY SPIRIT BEING RELEASED WITHIN ME. HOW FAITHFUL HE IS TO REVEAL AND HEAL. I CANNOT PRAISE HIM ENOUGH.

In another, I was walking down a slanted sidewalk. Immediately, I was on what I'll call the shadow side of heaven—there was a division line between brilliant light and dark shadows. When I looked up, I could see the brilliant light of heaven. The hand of God came over the division line and touched me. I was instantly drained of all strength. I fell on my face from His gentle touch.

The Lord then spoke saying, "From this day forth, you shall prophesy as never before."

I responded out of the weakness of my soul by saying, "O God, I am already in trouble with people for prophesying."

After I repented, I did prophesy more than before as well as sing prophetically.

I was at a conference where a prophet began to call people out and give them a word from the Lord. On the way home I said to the Lord, "I wished he would have prophesied over me."

The Lord answered, "Patt, you could prophesy over yourself." Anytime the Lord speaks to your heart, you are enabled and empowered to do what He says--that is His grace. I was truly given the ability to prophesy over myself, but my faith was weak. In Ezekiel 37, the Lord shows Ezekiel the valley of dry bones and asked him to prophesy over what He saw—so he did. But I didn't do what the Lord said I could do.

I said, "I know I have the ability in Christ to do so, but I wouldn't want my flesh to get in the way."

That night I had a dream. The prophet from the conference came up behind me, laid his hands on my shoulders and said, "You have been given a 'pointed' ministry."

I awoke from the dream and knew the Lord had the prophet pray over me.

Years later, when I was worshiping the Lord, I heard Him say, "You have an 'acute' ministry." I looked up the definition of acute to make sure I understood what He as saying. As you probably know, it means sharp-pointed. He was reaffirming the words the prophet prayed over me in that dream.

In January of 1981, I dreamed I was pregnant with something God wanted to birth. Its due date was 12/24/81. At that time, I had no understanding as to its meaning. I forgot about this dream until years later when I was reading my old dream journal.

Late summer of 1981, I had another dream. I saw the calendar turn from September to October to November and on to December. I could see around December 25th, there was light shining and spilling over to the days around it. In the dream, the phone rang. When I answered it, this man whom we had never met said, "Our group has gotten together and are in agreement that Milo and you are to be our pastors."

I thought I understood this dream since we had left the denominational church we had served in for ten years. We were looking for somewhere to pastor. There had been two different churches that had wanted us to pastor. The first one decided we were not the ones they wanted after all. The second church told us they wanted us to come in the fall. So, we were sure it was the church God wanted us to pastor. September came and that church called to tell us that the previous Sunday another couple had walked in and they were their new pastors. I became angry with God. I believed He had reneged.

We had friends from Australia coming to visit the week of Christmas. After dinner we started talking. We had not said one word to them about our pastoring situation. Later, the woman said she wanted to prophesy over us individually. She prophesied over Milo and

> I HAD FALLEN INTO THE SIN OF PRESUMPTION WHICH WAS DEVASTATING TO MY SOUL.

then came to me. She was really shaking from the anointing on her.

She placed her hands on my head and said, "It shall surely come to pass just as I, the Lord have spoken it to your heart."

Then she repeated it a second time, "It shall surely come to pass just as I, the Lord have spoken it to your heart."

I said within my heart, "And just how are You going to do that, Lord?"

I had a really bad attitude after all that had transpired, but then on December 24, the phone rang.

When I answered it, I heard a man say, "Our group has gotten together and are in agreement that Milo and you are to be our pastors."

Of course, we accepted that call as it was exactly as the Lord spoke it to me in the dream. I learned so much from this dream about presumption and its fruit. I had great remorse and have diligently sought to not fall into presumption again.

> *Keep back thy servant also from presumptuous sins; let them not have dominion over me!* (Psalm 19:13 RSV)

> *Watch out for false prophets. They come to you in sheep's clothing, but inwardly they are ferocious wolves. By their fruit you will recognize them.* (Matthew 7:15-16 NIV)

While praying, I saw a wolf and I heard the Lord say, "Protection is only found in Me."

Biblically, the wolf is depicted as a false prophet who comes in sheep's clothing, i.e. having the appearance of a Christian. Wolves come to rob, kill or deceive the weak ones.

One time, a pastor came to give me a word of correction because he believed I was rebellious. I told him that I knew I didn't have a rebellious spirit because from the time I was a small girl my thinking was, "Why don't people obey, then they wouldn't get in so much trouble."

This pastor became so full of rage that he drew his fist back to hit me. His hand stopped in midair. I believe it was the invisible hand of God stopping him. I looked over at his wife and her face showed total shock. If I had been screaming and yelling at him, I might not have been surprised, but his action totally shocked me.

Repeated Dreams and Snap Dreams

*Joseph replied to Pharaoh, "**It is not within my power, but God will speak concerning the welfare of Pharaoh**." Then Pharaoh said to Joseph, "In my dream I was standing by the edge of the Nile. Then seven fat and fine-looking cows were coming up out of the Nile, and they grazed in the reeds. Then seven other cows came up after them; they were scrawny, very bad-looking, and lean. I had never seen such bad-looking cows as these in all the land of Egypt! The lean, bad-looking cows ate up the seven fat cows. When they had eaten them, no one would have known that they had done so, for they were just as bad-looking as before. Then I woke up. I also saw in my dream seven heads of grain growing on one stalk, full and good. Then seven heads of grain, withered and thin and burned with the east wind, were sprouting* *up after them. The thin heads of grain swallowed up the seven good heads of grain. So I told all this to the diviner-priests, but no one could tell me its meaning."*

*Then Joseph said to Pharaoh, **"Both dreams of Pharaoh have the same meaning.** God has revealed to Pharaoh what he is about to do. The seven good cows represent seven years, and the seven good heads of grain represent seven years. Both dreams have the same meaning. The seven lean, bad-looking cows that came up after them represent seven years, as do the seven empty heads of grain burned with the east wind. They represent seven years of famine. This is just what I told Pharaoh: God has shown Pharaoh what he is about to do. Seven years of great abundance are coming throughout the whole land of Egypt. But seven years of famine will occur after them, and all the abundance will be forgotten in the land of Egypt. The famine will devastate the land. The previous abundance of the land will not be remembered because of the famine that follows, for the famine will be very severe. The dream was* *repeated to Pharaoh because the matter has been decreed by God, and God will make it happen soon.* (Genesis 41:16-32 NET emphasis mine)

One night, I had what I call a **Snap Dream**. It is when one sees a single picture like a snapshot or a few seconds of a video. In this **Snap Dream**, I saw a money clip with currency clipped in it. I went back to sleep, but I did not remember it in the morning.

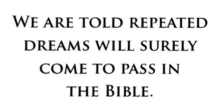

WE ARE TOLD REPEATED DREAMS WILL SURELY COME TO PASS IN THE BIBLE.

However, that afternoon I was resting in my chair and drifted off to sleep. I saw the same **Snap Dream**. I immediately woke up remembering it was the same as the one I had the night before. Since God had repeated it, I knew the Lord was saying there was money coming our way.

About two weeks later, a woman handed my husband and me seven one-hundred-dollar bills. I was shocked, but then I remembered the Lord had said money was coming. It met a need I hadn't even realized we had.

Our Father has knowledge of your needs even before you make your requests to him. (Matthew 6:8 BBE)

One night I was awakened with a great urgency to pray for our son, Michael. Silently, I prayed in the Spirit for a long time. When peace flooded my soul, I started singing within myself, "How great is His goodness stored up for those who fear Him… hidden away, hidden from harm. How great His love."[2] I drifted off to sleep and had a **Snap Dream** of what looked like the side of a hill that had slid down to the base of the hill.

The next morning while having devotions, the phone rang. I answered and it was our son.

His first words were, "Mom, I am alright."

I responded with, "Why wouldn't you be alright?"

He said, "We just had an earthquake here in California. I just wanted you and Dad to know I am okay."

After the call, I turned on the TV to see what they would be showing concerning the earthquake. The first picture I saw was the exact picture I had seen in the **Snap Dream**. Our son had truly been hidden away from harm. God's love, assurance, and foretelling are so amazing.

One spring day our young daughter, Susan, had misplaced the Mickey Mouse watch her grandparents had given her for Christmas. She had looked everywhere and could not find it. She was really upset, so I looked through everything in the house and in every room to no avail. Then one night, I had a **Snap Dream.** I was cleaning the house and I found the watch.

Although the **Snap Dream** said I would find the watch, I didn't look for it again. Then one day, I happen to hit the ruffle around the lower edge of the lamp shade and her watch fell out. We had a very happy daughter.

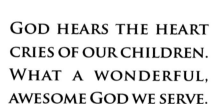

GOD HEARS THE HEART CRIES OF OUR CHILDREN. WHAT A WONDERFUL, AWESOME GOD WE SERVE.

In 2001, I dreamed and saw the back of an eagle sitting on a spindly branch. Then the branch broke, but the eagle still clung to the broken branch falling sideways. It never put out its wings to fly. I wondered why it was perched on a branch and why it would not try to fly when it broke.

This is what the Lord says: "Cursed is the one who trusts in man, who depends on flesh for his strength and whose heart turns away from the Lord." (Jeremiah 17:5 NIV)

I knew the eagle represented the United States. Wood has always represented the flesh of man to me. The branch the eagle was holding onto represents our nation's desire to hold on to the earthly things. We have trusted our own power and abilities to protect ourselves for far too long. The eagle's fall revealed a big fall was coming to the United States. We did see that fall with the economic bust in the mid-2000s.

My prayer has always been for the Lord to open our eyes and ears to His call with humility, brokenness, and repentance.

In December of 2006, I dreamed someone had placed two death wreaths on my door. I knew that was a custom practiced when someone in the family died. So, I was relatively certain that there would be two deaths not very far apart in my family. Now that was not a shock as my Mom was ninety-five at the time of this dream. I just didn't know who the other one might be. In 2007, my oldest sister's battle with lung cancer escalated. In October of 2007, she passed away. Exactly one month later, my Mother passed away. Both knew the Lord, so I am certain I will see them again. The Lord is so gracious to prepare us for what is to come.

In the late 1970s, I dreamed I was told to go up to the top floor of this skyscraper. I started up and then descend a few steps. Then I started up again and went a little higher than before, but descended a few steps again. This was repeated until I finally got to the top. At the top, the building was swaying and I was frightened. Upon awakening, my adrenalin was racing.

The dream could mean that I had started to do what the Lord told me to, but I had become frightened by what it required. I wasn't sure at the time. However, in the last few years I had a very similar dream. In this dream, I was already on the top floor of a skyscraper. I had no fear. In fact, the building was swaying and the winds were violent. There was great turbulence and debris was flying around outside the windows. I still had no fear. I knew this was the end, but I was safe in Jesus. Through the years, I have gone from fear to trust and faith. I now agree with Psalm 91. I am safe in Him.

Then in late 2012, I dreamed I was high up in a skyscraper and there were three weird-shaped planes flying directly toward the floor I was on. Instantly, I began falling

> IT CAUSED ME TO BE MORE VIGILANT IN SPIRITUAL WARFARE, AS I REALIZED IT COULD BE A SEQUEL TO THE 9/11 TRAGEDY.

amid the debris. I awakened with my whole body tingling with adrenalin. Since I was awake, I told my husband my dream. Then I drifted off to sleep and dreamed the whole thing over again, except this time I saw the planes and the skyscraper on a TV. I tried to tell my husband my dream again only to realize I was still asleep.

In the late 1980s, I also dreamed I was at a checkout counter. As I looked down, I saw there was a $100 bill on the floor. I was shocked that no one had picked it up. The shock almost caused me to pass out.

When I told Milo about my dream, he found it interesting. He had forgotten that as a child his parents had purchased a $100 savings bond for him. This dream was fulfilled a few weeks later when his parents sent the savings bond to him. He redeemed it for over $250. I was shocked

GOD IS SO TIMELY AND GRACIOUS. HE IS TO BE GLORIOUSLY PRAISED.

because I never even knew he had a savings bond. It met a need we had at the time.

Years ago, I dreamed I was at a hospital as a visitor and for some reason they accidently gave me a sonogram. I was surprised when they told me I was pregnant and it was a boy. I responded with, "His name is David." [End of dream]

Pregnant can also be defined as being prepared for something of great importance or potential. I knew I would not have a physical baby, so I just put this on the shelf to see if the Lord would reveal its meaning later.

A few years after this dream, a woman called to ask if my prayer partner and I would please come and pray over their lives and their home. She told me of all the cultic things they had been involved in, so we consented to go.

When we arrived at their home, we used our God-given authority as revealed in Matthew 28:19-20 and Mark 16:17-18, to cast out all the demonic powers they had invited into their lives and their home. This woman and her husband then started attending our church.

One Sunday, the Holy Spirit began to move mightily. Several people were slain in the Spirit; one was this woman's husband. When he started to get up, the Lord held him down. Again, he tried to get up only to be held down by the power of God. This was repeated a few more times. He started laughing because the Lord

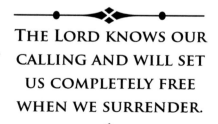

THE LORD KNOWS OUR CALLING AND WILL SET US COMPLETELY FREE WHEN WE SURRENDER.

had such a hold on him that all he could do was surrender. I believe this man was the baby I called "David" in my dream. Today, this couple is pastoring young people.

I dreamed I had prepared steaks and hamburgers for our church people. A few days later, I opened my oven and realized the people had left all the meat in the oven on warm. I had presumed they had eaten all the meat. They hadn't so now the meat was worthless. The people had only straightened up my kitchen to give the appearance that all the meat had been consumed. So it is with many "church people" today. They have no hunger for God's meat, i.e. His Word.

This dream revealed that one may prepare the meat of the Word, but it doesn't mean people will eat. Many just give an appearance of eating the Word of God. This action results in not hearing the Lord because the Word and the Lord are one (see John 1:1).

In the early 1980s, I dreamed I would live to see the last great outpouring of God, but my friend Bobbie would not. My friend was only two years older than me, but she passed away twenty years ago. I do not know why God gives me dreams about people dying. Possibly, it is a time table in my life. I always pray for the ones whose deaths are foretold. I pray that they complete their destiny in Christ.

In the late 1990s, I dreamed that all my nine living siblings would die before me. There were only two of us left in the dream and the remaining sibling was wounded for being a Christian. Since the time of that dream, I have had six

GOD HEARS AND ANSWERS. HOW COMFORTING AND AWESOME! I SEE GOD'S FAITHFULNESS EVERY DAY.

siblings pass away. Only three siblings are alive today. I have prayed for each of my siblings to truly know Jesus as their Savior. I believe I will see all of them again.

And if we know that he hears us—whatever we ask—we know that we have what we asked of him. (1 John 5:15 NIV)

I dreamed the Lord was presenting me with a large medallion, similar to an Olympic medal. I didn't understand this dream or why He would be giving me a medal.

Later, I understood that I was being rewarded for obtaining victory over the troubled times I went through as a result of having fear and an incorrect perception of my Dad. In essence, I perceived God as being like my earthly father. As a result of my wrong thinking, I believed there was something wrong with me.

Some of the incorrect God concepts I had were:

- *God has favorites like my Dad did and I am not one of them.*
- *God will not protect me from false accusations as my Dad hadn't.*
- *God will provide for others, but not for me.*
- *God is good to everyone except me.*
- *God punishes me for the slightest infraction, but ignores the wrongs of others.*
- *I had to be perfect to be acceptable to God. Knowing I wasn't perfect caused me to believe I would never be acceptable.*
- *I fail to please God, just like I failed to please my Dad.*

I renewed my mind by finding the root of each lie concerning each incorrect perception. God revealed the truth of how He saw each situation and that brought me peace. Then I had to replace the lie with the truth as God saw it. This caused me to grow in Christ and become more like Him.

I give thanks to my Lord for His grace that enabled me to truly see Father God as He truly is, and not from the perspective of my earthly father. God is good and loves me no matter what the situation. His love is not based on my performance. I thank God for His patience and perseverance to work in me until I came to believe God is good all the time.

> *When the ground soaks up the falling rain and bears a good crop for the farmer, it has God's blessing. But if a field bears thorns and thistles, it is useless. The farmer will soon condemn that field and burn it.* (Hebrews 6:7-8 NLT)

I want my life to be fruitful for Christ. When I studied the book of Esther, I learned she had to spend months in preparation before she was able to go before an earthly king. How much more should we be diligent in preparing our hearts for the King of kings? Esther was prepared with perfumes and oils. We need

WE NEED TO TOTALLY SURRENDER TO OUR LOVING HEAVENLY FATHER, KNOWING HE HAS ONLY THE BEST PLAN IN PLACE FOR US.

the oil of the Holy Spirit so we are able to remove the stench of the world's perfume and the smell of our flesh.

Surrendering to Our Heavenly Father

We will begin to understand our God-given dreams and words when we surrender our mind, will, emotions, and all thinking that rises up against the knowledge of God.

I would encourage you to pursue Him for the understanding of your dream(s). God knows all. He understands how you think and He loves to have His children commune with Him.

Perhaps, though, you are like me and perceived God as being like your earthly father. As a result of my wrong thinking, I believed there was something wrong with me.

Look at this list of the incorrect God concepts I had and check any that you have received into your life.

- ☐ God has favorites like my Dad did and I am not one of them.
- ☐ God will not protect me from false accusations as my Dad hadn't.
- ☐ God will provide for others, but not for me.
- ☐ God is good to everyone except me.
- ☐ God punishes me for the slightest infraction, but ignores the wrongs of others.

☐   I had to be perfect to be acceptable to God. Knowing I wasn't perfect caused me to believe I would never be acceptable.

☐   I fail to please God, just like I failed to please my Dad.

I renewed my mind by finding the root of each lie concerning my incorrect perceptions of my Heavenly Father. God revealed the truth of how He saw each situation and that brought peace into my life. When I replaced the lie with the truth as God saw it, it caused me to grow in Christ and become more like Him. What He did for me He will do for you. Just ask Him!

Pray: *Father God, I pray to have hearing ears and a hunger and a thirst for Your Word. May I truly desire the meat of Your Word so I will grow up into the godly person You have called me to be? Help me to overcome the lies and incorrect perceptions I have carried into adulthood, so I can fulfill the mission You have for me during my time here on earth. Thank You, Father God, for Your great love and patience in my life.*

Chapter 4

Visions

About thirty-five years ago, I was praying, but I wasn't hearing God speaking. I wondered why.

Then the Lord spoke to my heart saying, "If you would just pay attention to the pictures you are seeing with your spiritual eyes, you would have your answer."

We truly serve an all-knowing and creative God. Who desires to talk to each of us.

I then started paying attention to the pictures He was giving. Sure enough, the answer was in the pictures He was giving. To this day, I still see pictures (mini-visions) when I pray and/or worship Him. It amazes me that He speaks to me this way. All I can do is praise Him.

In the early 1990's, I was watching Benny Hinn on TV. He was giving out words of knowledge concerning different ones in his audience and what was in their lives. It angered me because I knew I had a problem, but could not find deliverance.

I stood up and walked into my kitchen saying, "If someone would tell me what my problem is I will deal with it."

Immediately, a vision appeared before my eyes. I could see everything in my kitchen, but I also saw an unending line of people. I was bowing before and worshiping each one of them because I feared their rejection, taunts, and judgments. I knew within my heart they were people I either perceived had rejected or judged me. I had a terror of them and their ability to hurt me.

Seeing this, I instantly knew I was in idolatry and had a spirit of rejection. I lacked the knowledge of God's goodness. I had always said God is good, but I had a little postscript in my heart that said, "To everyone except for me." This vision brought godly sorrow which led to deep repentance. I knew I was instantly delivered

ONLY JESUS CAN CHANGE OUR WRONG THINKING AND DELIVER US IN ONE OR TWO SECONDS. PTL!

for even my thinking changed. I knew I would never be harassed by rejection again and I haven't been.

However, it took about four years to renew my thinking concerning the lies I had believed about God, i.e. the wrong perceptions of my Dad I had projected onto God. All praise and glory goes to my Lord and Savior Jesus Christ.

Early in 2006, while I was in worship, Jesus showed me I had mail in my mail box. I opened the box and there was a package. I opened it. It was a zipped bank bag with a number on it. I unzipped it. It was full of currency.

This vision was fulfilled one month later. My sister, Mary had died from a blood clot to the lungs as a result of an accidental fall. Later that year, Mary's estate attorney sent me a check. The number of his check was the same as the number I saw on the bank bag. I had inherited a few thousand dollars.

Mary's death left a hole in my heart, but Jesus healed it as I sought Him. Money could not replace her, but these are the lyrics to the song He gave me that evening:

Awesome Holy Jesus
You're enthroned in majesty
Your voice peals forth like thunder
Establishing Your authority
I bow in surrender
To acknowledge You as Lord
I see You in Your glory
And in Your majesty
Awesome Holy Jesus
Sovereign King of Kings
You're worthy of all worship
Every knee will bow
Every tongue will confess
You are Lord

In 1997, while praying I saw a vision of a horse in a stall. There were straps attached to each side of her neck that connected to the stall walls. The purposes of the straps were to keep the horse stationary. Then the mane on the right side was lifted up and an injection was given. This caused the horse to instantly fall asleep, while still standing.

I began to pray and I heard the Lord say, "This is the American church. Satan has injected the church with sleep and she is not aware of what is about to come upon her. She has catered to earthly things rather than the God who established her as a Christian nation."

Having been around a lot of rodeos as a child, I have always seen the horse as something wild and unruly, i.e. rebellious. America is definitely acting like an unruly horse by giving up morality, truth and love for one another.

ARE YOU SLUMBERING? DID THE COLUMBINE SCHOOL SHOOTING IN 1999 AWAKEN YOU? DID 9-11 AWAKEN YOU TO SEEK GOD MORE? HAVE YOU CONTINUED TO PRAY AND STAY ALERT? WILL THE LORD FIND YOU ASLEEP AND WITHOUT FAITH WHEN HE RETURNS?

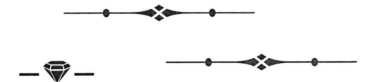

I saw the chair the Lord has assigned me in order to fulfill my calling in Him. There was a wastebasket

LORD, TEACH ME PATIENCE. I KNOW YOU HAVE AN APPOINTED TIME FOR ALL THINGS.

on the seat. I removed the basket, sat down, and began to knit.

The basket represented what holds waste.

I felt the Lord say, "You think waiting is a waste of time. Be still and wait patiently. I will call you at the appointed time."

Jesus took me to a cliff. I could see a dark city with a few lights shining.

He said, "I am going to send you to these cities to take My light to them."

I thought it looked like one city, and then I heard the Lord respond to my thinking saying, "These are cities within a city. The city

LORD, OPEN OUR HEARTS TO REACH OUT AND TOUCH THOSE LOST IN THE CITY OF DARKNESS.

of hunger, the city of the lost, the city of the needy, the city of the sick, the city of poverty and wanting, and the city of hopelessness. All these cities are in this city of darkness."

I see the Lord and He put His arms around me and pointed and said, "Let's go."

What I saw was the U.S and she was like a wild bucking horse.

The Lord said, "She is trying to throw off what is coming upon her, but she cannot. She must reap what she has sown."

Then the Lord turned to me and personally said, "I am going to preserve you, because of your obedience to Me. Fear not, for I am with you and will be with you to the end. I will keep you. Those who have repented of their rebellion I will also keep safe."

While praying, I saw Jesus wearing safety welding glasses, driving a wagon pulled by a rebellious horse kicking up dirt.

Because I was wondering about this, the Lord said, "The rebellious will try to kick dirt in My face as well as yours, but trust Me. I AM the One who guards. I AM your refuge and high tower who protects and shields you. I will keep you safe. Your vision will not be thwarted. Trust Me, I AM God."

I understood this to mean that there are people who will proclaim what I see and heard are wrong. However, God is my fortress and high tower.

In 2001, while praying I could see a puffy cloud and on it was written NEO. [I had no idea what that acronym meant nor did the Lord tell me. So, I searched out its meaning and felt **New Economic Order** agreed with the picture.] Beside the acronym, I saw a pipe barely dripping water or oil. Written next to the pipe was the phrase, *Net Dollar.* Next to that phrase, I saw a galvanized pail with two horseshoes hooked over the edge of it. The Lord took the pail and horseshoes and threw them into His fire.

I know the Lord's fire is to cleanse and purify. I knew the pail was an alloy, which represented things that are man-made, worldly, and tainted. The Lord told me the horseshoes represented luck, which has deceived America and mankind. They think luck is on their side and things will get better and better, but their pail was empty. Many are empty of God.

LORD, OPEN THE EYES OF YOUR PEOPLE.
BRING US TO TRUE REPENTANCE THAT KNOWS YOU ALONE ARE GOD.
TRUE PROSPERITY, HEALTH, AND WEALTH COME FROM YOU ALONE.

I really didn't understand the full meaning of this vision until after the collapse of the money market in 2006. Then I understood what the Lord was telling me—all that man trusted would be lost with little left.

The Lord Himself is to be our provision, security, our Rock, our Fortress, our Salvation, and our Hope.

> *The Lord is my rock and my fortress and my deliverer; My God, my strength, in whom I will trust; My shield and the horn of my salvation, my stronghold. 3 I will call upon the Lord, who is worthy to be praised; So shall I be saved from my enemies.* (Psalm 18:2-3 NKJV)

Our son-in-law, Randy, was working for Micron in the early 2000s. Micron's stock was the lowest I had ever seen it.

My daughter called and said, "Mom, will you please pray. Micron is so bad Randy is concerned about losing his job."

ISN'T IT WONDERFUL HOW GOD SHOWS HIS POWER AND HIS CARE FOR US?

I said, "Yes." I went to prayer and saw Micron was a dead bird in the Lord's hands.

The Lord asked me, "Can this dead bird fly?"

I responded, "Yes, all things are possible with You."

The Lord then lifted His hands and the bird flew away, very alive. Then I knew that Micron would be revived and it was. It's thriving now.

One of my friends asked me to pray that the Lord would provide the finances they needed to go to Bible School. As I prayed, I could see the Lord pouring out currency over them from an airplane. Weeks later, she informed me that the finances had come in like a windfall.

> **THE LORD ALWAYS SEES THE NEEDS OF HIS PEOPLE AND IF THEY BELIEVE HE INTERVENES ON THEIR BEHALF. PTL!**

In worship one morning, the Lord gave me a bag of gold nuggets. The bag was real heavy. I took one nugget out of the sack and gave it to Jesus, not knowing why. I immediately felt I had given Him so little. I asked Jesus to forgive me for being selfish.

He said, "It is a tithe."

A few weeks later, while I was in worship I saw Jesus with a cup of steaming hot coffee. He opened my bag of gold nuggets and poured the coffee over the gold nuggets.

In my spirit I understood He was calling me to awaken those who are falling asleep. He wants His people to come to attention and seek His Word, will and holiness.

Wake up O sleeper, rise from the dead, and Christ will shine on you. (Ephesians 5:14 NIV)

One Sunday toward the end of the song service, the Lord appeared before me with a red rose in His hand.

CHERISH THAT WHICH IS ETERNAL.

He handed it to me saying, "This is from Me to you."

The song service ended and one of the elders went to the front and said, "This is the Sunday we honor the pastor's wife. Patt, will you please come forward."

I went up and was given a money gift.

I was thankful for their gift and I knew the people thought it was a gift from them. However, I understood the Lord was saying their gift was from Him also.

The love of the Lord is more valuable and precious than the words and gifts of man. The love of the Lord satisfies our hearts forever, while the gifts of people are temporary and sometimes forgotten.

"For what is seen is temporary, but what is unseen is eternal." (2 Corinthians 4:18 NIV)

There was a large wooden Cross on the wall behind the pulpit in one of the churches we pastored. When Milo stood to preach, the crossbar of the cross could be seen above his head. In this vision, I looked up at the cross and huge doves begin to fly out into the sanctuary. One landed on Milo's head. I was impressed the Holy Spirit was descending on the service. The sanctuary was then filled with flying doves.

LORD, MAY ALL WHO ARE RESISTING YOU BE CONVICTED AND REALIZE THE TRUTH AND VALUE OF HOLY SPIRIT.

As I looked around, I saw some of the doves landed on some of the congregation. Others were flailing with their hands to keep the doves from settling down upon them.

A melody started running through my head, "There's a river of life flowing out of me...opens prison doors, sets the captives free."[3]

A few months after this vision, it was fulfilled in our regular Sunday service. After Pastor's sermon about the Holy

Spirit's work in our lives, I could see in the Spirit realm huge doves flying out of the Cross. The doves were trying to alight upon all the heads of the people. Some allowed Holy Spirit to settle upon them and some were flailing their hands to keep Holy Spirit from landing.

I was saddened. I found it hard to believe that any Christian would resist the Holy Spirit and His power that enables us to live a victorious life.

While praying, I could see I was in a cemetery. There was a grave stone with a church's name on it. The Lord revealed this church was dead and basically buried. Within three months, that church closed its doors.

I prayed for the resurrection power of God to invade their midst. The people at that church said they knew it was the Lord's will to close. However, I was saddened that they had not embraced the resurrection power of God that was needed to keep their church alive.

In 1993, I could see I was walking on a path with Jesus. He said, "He that hath an ear, let him hear."

I asked the Lord what He wanted me to hear. At that moment, I saw there was a mail-wrapped package tied with a string. I cut the string and opened the package. It was a ream of paper.

I then heard, "I want you to write."

I asked, "What do You want me to write?"

"I will show you," was His answer.

As I was praying, I saw Jesus before me. I understood He wanted me to follow Him. He opened a small trap door and descended, so I followed Him. Instantly, I could see huge orange and yellow flames everywhere. I could see people in the flames, but they were not close enough to speak to them. I knew within myself that these were people falling into hell.

This vision immediately sent me to prayer for those who were not ready to meet their maker. I knew they were headed for a horrible eternity. May God's word go out and touch the hearts of all who are resisting Him and those negligent in their relationship with the Lord.

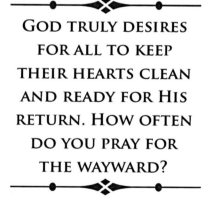

GOD TRULY DESIRES FOR ALL TO KEEP THEIR HEARTS CLEAN AND READY FOR HIS RETURN. HOW OFTEN DO YOU PRAY FOR THE WAYWARD?

In the spirit realm, I could see a gun barrel come from behind a corner. It was pointed at me. I rebuked Satan in the name of Jesus and it drew back around the corner. This was repeated two more times. The last time a bullet came right at me, but Jesus put out His hand and caught the bullet. Then He sent it back in the direction from which it came.

This revealed there was someone who was coming against me with words of judgment. I prayed for this person to be blessed with God's love and truth that brings repentance. Jesus' action reassured me that He is always present to protect. It also told me not to receive any words that did not agree with His Word.

THANK YOU, LORD FOR ALWAYS BEING PRESENT TO WATCH OVER AND PROTECT YOUR PEOPLE.

Jesus putting out His hand to catch the bullet caused me to remember two scripture verses:

Do not be deceived, God is not mocked; for whatever a man sows, that he will also reap. (Galatians 6:7 NKJV)

"Vengeance is Mine, I will repay," says the Lord. (Romans 12:19 NKJV)

*The godly are rescued from trouble, and it falls
on the wicked instead.* (Proverbs 11:8 NLT)

In 2008, while I was worshiping the Lord, I could see He had a globe of the earth in His hand. He set it down on a table and gave the globe a spin. Then He put His finger out, stopping it on the Northern countries of Africa. I wondered why and what He wanted me to pray about concerning that area, but He gave no directives. So, I prayed the best I knew how, but felt that was inadequate. Only when the Arab Uprising started in 2010, did I really understand the great need to pray for the countries in northern Africa.

The Lord took my hand and said, "'Hang on. You should never let go because you are never to be independent of Me. I will never let go of you, so never let go of Me. No one, absolutely no one can pull you away from Me."

WHAT THE LORD SAID TO ME HE SAYS TO ALL BELIEVERS. TAKE HIS HAND AND BELIEVE.

For He has said, "I will never leave you nor forsake you." (Hebrews 13:5 NKJV)

The Lord took me to a waterfall which represents the flowing of God's Spirit. A huge black thing on the waterfall was hindering the water from flowing.

The Lord said, "I am going to remove all that is not of Me.".

Then I saw the black thing being ripped away from top to bottom. Next, I saw the Lord picking up eight to ten-inch stones from the water.

I asked the Lord, "Why are you picking up the stones?"

He answered, "These are my diamonds in the rough. I am going to cut and polish them, so they will bring forth My light and My beauty."

The stones then begin to sparkle and move like the northern lights—revealing God's beauty and His creation.

The Lord said, *"My Light will draw many, but there are others who will be repelled by it."* *Everyone who does evil hates the light, and will not come into the light for fear that his deeds will be exposed. 21 But whoever lives by the truth comes into the light, so that it may be seen plainly that what he has done has been done through God.* (John 3:20-21 NIV)

While praying, I put my head on Father's knee.

He hugged me and said, "You are always welcome here."

Father is not a respecter of persons, so this is true for you also.

> *Come before His presence with singing. Know that the Lord, He is God; It is He who has made us, and not we ourselves; We are His people and the sheep of His pasture.* (Psalm 100:2-3 NKJV)

While worshipping the Lord, He handed me a bag of gold dust.

Then He said, "My gold is within you. My gold dust is not just to be sprinkled over you. It must dwell within you."

MAY EVERY BELIEVER HUNGER AND THIRST FOR MORE OF HIS QUALITIES.

I knew the gold represented His Word, truth, holiness, and promises. Therefore, I understand we are not to merely have an outward covering of God's qualities, but His character must dwell within each of us.

> *"The Lord does not look at the things man looks at. Man looks at the outward appearance, but the Lord looks at the heart."* (1 Samuel 16:7 NIV)

While praying, I saw myself as an airplane carrying a mailbag on one of its wings. The mailbag started to slip off. This concerned me for I didn't want to lose what belonged to someone else. Then I see the second handle of the mailbag was being placed over the other wing. The mailbag was then secure.

I understood this to mean that none of the visions, prophetic words or words God spoke to my heart would be lost. The Lord was reassuring me that He would secure His breathed words in my heart and at the appointed time He would show me the ones to whom the words belong. I would not lose any mail.

> *So shall My word be that goes forth from My mouth; It shall not return to Me void,*

But it shall accomplish what I please, And it shall prosper in the thing for which I sent it. (Isaiah 55:11 NKJV)

I was sitting next to Jesus who was seated on His throne. One of His children was dancing before us. Her dance was calling people to come and commune with Him for He is worthy. I could sense the

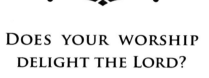

DOES YOUR WORSHIP DELIGHT THE LORD?

Lord was delighted by the worship. I decided to join her in the dance.

In January of 1997, I saw two hands join in agreement. As they were joining their hands, I could see an army tank about to encroach upon America. Next, I saw the words, **"War of Hatred."**

The Lord said, "It is at hand."

I prayed the only way I knew how, but I did not pray enough concerning this. I do think it was pointing to the Columbine massacre, twin towers attack, the Arab Uprising, ISIS, and all the hatred coming forth now.

Two weeks after the last entry, I saw a pipe clogged with mud.

The Lord said, "This is what the people who call themselves My Church are like. Therefore, I have attached to this pipe what is needed so the flesh will be removed. If My people will submit to what I have ordained by repenting, there will be a cleansing from all that is defiling them."

HAS THE WATER PRESSURE
OF GOD'S WORD PURGED
YOUR UNGODLY DESIRES?
ARE YOU REVEALING JESUS TO
THE WORLD AND ESPECIALLY
TO THOSE AROUND YOU?

———●——◆——●———

I DO BELIEVE THAT IF WE COULD SEE THE FULLNESS OF HIS LOVE WE WOULD BE SO OVERWHELMED, ALL WE WOULD DO IS BOW AND WORSHIP OUR GOD OF UNCONDITIONAL LOVE.

———●——◆——●———

One pre-dawn morning, the Lord revealed to me the magnitude of His love.

He said, "My love is so vast that it is often unseen. When one stands a few feet from a tall and massive building, all one really sees is a small portion of the building. So, it is with My love."

I saw the Lord was pouring water on this beautiful vibrant white flower. The water caused a man looking like a black spider to crawl out.

This reveals God's desires to remove anything from our lives that hinders our walk with Him.

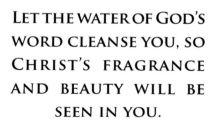

LET THE WATER OF GOD'S WORD CLEANSE YOU, SO CHRIST'S FRAGRANCE AND BEAUTY WILL BE SEEN IN YOU.

While praying, I saw myself driving in a small convertible on a treacherous road. The car was hugging the road and going very slow.

I heard the Lord say, "You need not fear. I am with you. I know where the exact edge of the road is."

I went around the curve and the road was only the width of the car. I proceeded confidently as I knew Jesus was with me. I knew I had no reason to fear. Before long, we were safely down in the valley.

This symbolized the road in my life was the treacherous journey I was experiencing at that time. The Lord was addressing the spider of fear that was threatening to keep me from moving forward.

ALL WE NEED TO DO
IS ACKNOWLEDGE
HIS PRESENCE.

He is so faithful to encourage us to keep going, no matter how rough the path may become.

God Gives Us Strength for the Journey

> *I can do everything through him who gives
> me strength.* (Philippians 4:13 NIV)

There are many powerful revelations, statements, and scriptures in this chapter that I would encourage you to take a few minutes to review before you move on to the next chapter. Record in your journal what you have gleaned from this chapter.

Do you believe we truly serve an all-knowing and creative God who desires to talk to each of us? _____ Why or why not? _____

Only Jesus can change our wrong thinking and deliver us. What do you need Him to deliver you of today? _____

_____

Did the Columbine school shooting in 1999 awaken you? _____

Did 9-11 awaken you to seek God more? _____

Have you continued to pray and stay alert or will the Lord find you asleep and without faith when He returns? _____

Pray: *Lord, open our hearts to reach out and touch those lost in the city of darkness. Lord, open the eyes of Your people. Bring us to repentance with the knowledge that You alone are the source of true prosperity, health, and wealth. Lord, may all who are resisting You be convicted and realize the truth and value of Holy Spirit. Thank You,*

Lord for always being present to watch over and protect Your people.

For He has said, "I will never leave you nor forsake you." (Hebrews 13:5 NKJV)

> *"My Light will draw many, but there are others who will be repelled by it." Everyone who does evil hates the light, and will not come into the light for fear that his deeds will be exposed. But whoever lives by the truth comes into the light, so that it may be seen plainly that what he has done has been done through God.* (John 3:20-21 NIV)

He is so faithful to encourage us to keep going no matter how rough the path may become. All we need to do is acknowledge His presence. What the Lord said to me He says to all believers. Take His hand and believe.

CHAPTER 5
WORDS THE LORD SPOKE TO MY HEART

A few months after I was saved, I had the distinct knowledge that someone I knew was going to die. Even though I had that knowledge, I did not know how to pursue the Lord to hear and understand what He was trying to tell me. Within three weeks, one of the neighbor's children died of appendicitis.

Within myself, I said, *Oh that must be what the Lord was saying.*

However, a couple of weeks later my dad died of a stroke at fifty-three. I didn't even understand enough to really pray as I should have.

GOD SPOKE, BUT I DIDN'T UNDERSTAND.

I heard the Lord say, "Hear My voice, Oh My people. There is a sound going forth that sounds like Mine, but it is not. Those who abide in Me hear and know My voice. It is important that you develop a discerning ear. Many times, another voice will appear to sound like Mine only to mislead you from sound truth. My voice will always bring peace to those who are hearing."

I will make peace your governor and righteousness your ruler. (Isaiah 60:17 NIV)

You [the Lord] *will keep in perfect peace him whose mind is steadfast, because he trusts in you.* (Isaiah 26:3 NIV)

The Lord said, "I am working on you daily to change you into my likeness. I love you."

For those whom He foreknew, He also predestined to become conformed to the image of His

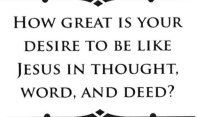

HOW GREAT IS YOUR DESIRE TO BE LIKE JESUS IN THOUGHT, WORD, AND DEED?

Son, so that He would be the firstborn among many brethren; and these whom He predestined, He also called; and these whom He called, He also justified; and these whom He justified, He also glorified. (Romans 8:29-30 NASB)

When I was about eight-years old, my stomach was hurting and I didn't know why.

I was trying to figure it out when I heard, "You haven't had a bowel movement for five days."

I thought, *That's right.*

I told Mom my problem and she gave me something to help. I don't know how I knew it was God speaking, but I did.

The Lord said, "My supply is never diminished by giving."

What an awesome thought. What God gives never decreases His supply.

HAVE YOU BEEN TAPPING INTO HIS VAST SUPPLY?

"I have come that they may have life, and that they may have it more abundantly." (John 10:10 NKJV)

The Lord said, "My hand is extended to My people with goodness and mercy. A humble and a contrite heart I will not despise. Just ask to be

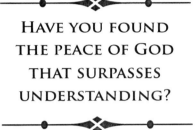

HAVE YOU FOUND THE PEACE OF GOD THAT SURPASSES UNDERSTANDING?

forgiven, and break your agreement with any judgments against yourself. Then peace will invade your heart."

In January of 1967, our eldest daughter, Susan, was two months old. My husband was working the swing shift at Hallmark Cards in Kansas City. Susan developed a temperature of 102 and I had no transportation to take her to the emergency room, nor did I know anyone to call.

In my distress, the Lord spoke to me saying, "Patt, you think this child is yours. She is not, she's Mine."

In that moment, I realized I really believed she was mine. I asked God to forgive me.

I said, "I now offer her back to You, Lord."

Susan's fever broke instantly. When our other two children were born, I immediately offered them back to the Lord.

In later years, I was able to share this with other mothers by saying, "When one goes to the library to borrow a book; the book never becomes yours. It is only on loan. The book has to be returned to the library just as we have to give ownership of our children back to the Lord. They belong to Him and we are to teach them to love the Lord, so when their return date comes they will be ready to meet their maker.

Back in the '90s a friend and I were passing a cemetery where a funeral service was in progress. I began to wonder when I would be standing over a grave.

I immediately heard the voice of the Lord say, "Your mother will lose a son and you will lose a brother."

Of course, one's mind would go to the eldest.

I saw my youngest brother, Steven, a few days after this word was given from the Lord. He told me that he had just had his yearly physical and was found healthy in all ways except they had upped his thyroid medicine. I was not prepared for the phone call I received two weeks later. My sister-in-law called saying that Steven had had a massive heart attack and died instantly. He was only forty-five.

I started screaming, "Lord, You told me, but I really did not seek You, because it seemed like it would be so far in the future. Forgive me, Lord of my presumption."

I really had a difficult time with Steven's death, but time and prayer brought healing to my soul.

The Lord said to me, "Today, we are going to do something special."

I sensed Satan was trying to push me in another direction than being quiet before the Lord. I bound and silenced the enemy using the authority God had given me. Power came out from the throne of God and paralyzed Satan.

While bowing before the throne of God, I start singing, "Safe am I in the hollow of His hands."[4] I knew I was safe in Jesus. The Lord said that He knows the future and the attacks Satan has planned, but He has given His people power to defeat the enemy of our souls.

HOW GREAT IS OUR GOD!

While in prayer the Lord said, "I Am the God of all peace! There is no peace without Me. All the world has is an appearance of peace."

Do you know the peace that surpasses understanding? There is no peace without Him. If you need peace run to Father God and tell Him your need.

THE PEACE OF GOD BRINGS DEEP REST.

One time the Lord asked me, "Have you touched My heart yet today?"

I answered, "I don't know, but You have touched mine simply by asking that question. What must I do to touch Your heart?"

I then saw a black circular thing covering some people. I knew within myself they were the people in the

HOW OFTEN DO YOU PRAY FOR THOSE WITHIN YOUR FELLOWSHIP AND THOSE WHO ARE NO LONGER IN YOUR SOCIAL CIRCLE?

church we were pastoring at the time and they needed prayer. I prayed for them and continue to pray for them when the Lord brings them to mind.

One day the Lord said to me, "The reason many have problems hearing Me is their flesh is speaking so loud they cannot hear My voice."

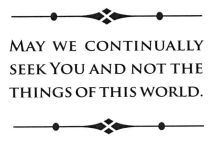

MAY WE CONTINUALLY SEEK YOU AND NOT THE THINGS OF THIS WORLD.

Help us, Lord to quiet our souls. Open our ears. Cause us to deal with any ungodly ambitions, appetites, and desires that keep us from hearing You.

Another time, I was fretting and stewing over the financial need we had.

Suddenly, the Lord spoke to my heart saying, "If you would just listen to the song playing on the radio, you will have the answer to your problem."

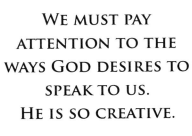

WE MUST PAY ATTENTION TO THE WAYS GOD DESIRES TO SPEAK TO US. HE IS SO CREATIVE.

I turned the radio up and the song playing was, "God will take care of you, through every day and all the way." All I could do is praise and worship the Lord. The next week we unexpectedly received a large sum of money that covered our needs. How wonderful and gracious is our all-knowing God!

The year I graduated from high school, I took a job. I was sure I was too dumb to pass English composition in college, even though I was in the upper 10 percent of my class out of sixty-six.

That summer, I asked the Lord when I would be married, and I heard, *"Four years."*

I remembered it, but didn't think about it. That summer, I met a young man I thought I wanted to marry and he asked me to marry him. When he left for the college in the fall, I had the distinct knowledge that there wouldn't be any more real interaction with him, even though, he said he would write. By Thanksgiving, I had not heard from him, so I called him long distance. He was furious to hear from me. A couple of weeks later, I received a "Dear John letter."

If only I'd had the wisdom to seek God concerning the distinct knowledge and whom He had planned for my life. God had spoken, but I didn't give it any credence.

One day long before that "Dear John letter" a young man came to church and sat down beside me.

As he did the Lord spoke very clearly to my spirit saying, "This is your husband."

I responded to the Lord within my heart, "'No, he's not, I am already engaged."

I later learned the young man's name was Milo. I promptly put that word out of my mind and I definitely did not pursue him.

Within a year, I was engaged to another young man. One day at an all dormitory meeting, Milo's sister was sitting across the room from me. I looked at her and again, I heard the Lord speak to my spirit as loudly as if He was standing beside me, "This is your sister-in-law."

Again, I said, "No, I'm engaged to W."

Before the year was out, I broke that engagement.

A couple of months later, Milo asked me out. It wasn't until the next fall that we began dating regularly. The following July, we were married. God had spoken four years and it was exactly four years when Milo and I married. God spoke, I heard, but I didn't listen very well. We have now been married for over fifty-two years.

In the first church we pastored, there was a man who tried to control everything that took place in the church. One Sunday, my fleshly nature got so aggravated that I told him off. The Lord began to talk to me about my attitude. He told me I needed to forgive the man and ask the man to forgive me.

I did recognize my wrong attitude and actions and asked God's forgiveness.

Then I told the Lord, "I will ask him to forgive me, but I will also tell him how wrong he is."

The Lord whispered to my heart, "An apology is not an apology if you reflect upon the wrong of the other. To rightly apologize, you must only reflect upon your own wrong doing."

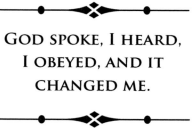

Following the Lord's correction, I changed what I was going to say. This word from the Lord has been a continuing guideline in my life.

GOD SPOKE, I HEARD, I OBEYED, AND IT CHANGED ME.

We later learned how much that man had also changed.

One day, I was reading Romans 12. I came to verse nine which says, "Love must be sincere. Hate what is evil; cling to what is good" (NIV).

I heard the precious voice of the Lord say, "Patt, you do not hate evil as I hate evil."

GOD IS SO WONDERFUL AND FAITHFUL TO SPEAK TO OUR HEARTS, SO WE WILL SEE SIN AS HE SEES SIN.

I agreed with the Lord. I didn't hate evil as He does. The Lord was very gracious to show me what I needed to change. I was convicted and repented. I started making other changes in my life.

I am very thankful He spoke this to my heart.

In the early 1980s, I was talking to another pastor's wife. She was telling me about giving a prophecy and being totally rebuked for it.

At that moment, the Lord spoke to my heart saying, "You are to go to such and such Church. I will give you a prophecy and you will be kicked for giving it."

I said, "Oh no, Lord, I don't want to do that."

I did not tell my husband because I didn't want to give a prophecy that would be rejected.

Since we were looking for a church, my husband suggested we go to such and such Church. It was the very one the Lord told me we were to attend.

I said, "Let's go to this other Church or this one or that other one."

My suggestions were to no avail. We went to such and such Church. I started praying silently in the Spirit and with English the moment we walked in. When I saw the pastor, I could tell he was a controller just by his actions, attitudes, and words. I continued praying silently through the service. The pastor made no room for any input from the Spirit of God until the end of the service. He took a breath and I gave the word the Lord had given me during the service. It was an encouraging prophecy about growing into mature eagles by learning to fly.

When I finished giving God's word, the pastor said, "That is a true word from God, but lady you are totally out of order."

I turned to my husband and asked, "Am I out of order?"

His response was, "The only one out of order is the pastor."

We never went there again.

About three years after this incident, a woman who had attended such and such Church stopped me and said, "The prophecy you gave at our church was right on and ministered to several of us in the church. The pastor had forbidden any of us to even talk to you."

> IN MINISTERING WE SOMETIMES MAKE MISTAKES, HOWEVER, GOD DESIRES FOR ALL TO BE HUMBLE AND REPENT, SO HE CAN USE US TO A GREATER DEGREE.

A few years later, I learned that pastor was no longer in the ministry.

About ten years ago, I was concerned for my youngest daughter's health and her weight. I began to pray that the Lord would cause her to see what she needed to do for better health. Time went by and I started petitioning the Lord again. More time passed and I prayed again.

This time the Lord said, "Patt, I heard you."

Instantly, I started praising the Lord as I knew He was referring to 1 John 5:14-15 which says, "This is the confidence we have in approaching God: that if we ask anything according to his will, he hears us. And if we know that he hears us—whatever we ask—we know that we have what we asked of him" (1 John 5:14-15 NIV).

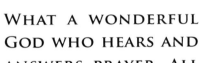

WHAT A WONDERFUL GOD WHO HEARS AND ANSWERS PRAYER. ALL GLORY GOES TO HIM.

A few months later, she was losing weight and her health improved.

While praying, the Lord gave me a violin to play. [In the natural I am not able to play any instrument.] As I begin to play it, there

WHEN THE MELODY OF HEAVEN GOES FORTH IT IS GOD'S CALL TO, "BE HOLY BECAUSE HE IS HOLY." LET US ALL RESPOND TO HIS CALL!

was a big black sheep that began to bow before the throne of God.

The Lord said, "When my sheep hear my call to holiness and respond they will go forth and do great exploits for their God."

I saw the Lord walking out the door with an old dull looking black sheep.

My question was, "Lord, what are You saying?"

He answered, "Here I am! I stand at the door and knock. If anyone hears my voice and opens the door, I will come in and eat with him, and he with me" (Revelation 3:20 NIV).

[This sheep had not asked the Lord to come into his life.]

The Lord said, "When I knock and you let Me into your life, it is so we can

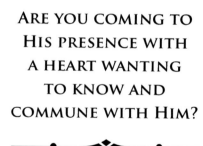

ARE YOU COMING TO HIS PRESENCE WITH A HEART WANTING TO KNOW AND COMMUNE WITH HIM?

commune with each other. When you come to My house [My Presence,] it is to be the same. However, many come for other reasons—to play, to have an emotional high, for social reasons, or appearances. But the day is coming when My house with be full of only those who desire to fellowship with Me."

One devotional time, I asked the Lord if there was something more He would like to share about Himself.

He then said, "I am a greenhouse—always pro-viding light, warmth, and the proper conditions for My people to grow. Those who spend time in My greenhouse will be in My presence. They will read

DO YOU SEE THE LORD AS YOUR GREENHOUSE? HOW MUCH TIME DO YOU SPEND IN HIS PRESENCE GETTING THE NOURISHMENT AND SPIRITUAL WATER YOU NEED FOR YOUR SPIRITUAL LIFE?

and love My Word. They will follow Me wherever I go."

I was looking at the first rose cut from my new rose bush and I heard the Lord say, "You are as beautiful to Me as that rose."

I asked "How can You love me so or see any beauty in me when I am so far from being like You?

He responded, I am love and I can only do, be, and give what I am."

I was so humbled and touched. This revealed to me I was judging myself.

Years ago, I saw the Lord in a wheelchair. I asked Him why He was in a wheelchair.

The Lord said, "Many of my people believe that I am handicapped by man's will. I am not, for My word declares, 'I know that you [my God] can do all things; no plan of yours can be thwarted'" (Job 42:2 NIV).

I know and believe that God never violates man's will, but I also know God has wonderful ways of working in us until we willingly follow His calling upon our lives, if we truly desire Him. Too often we think we know the will of God, but often it proves to be our own thinking.

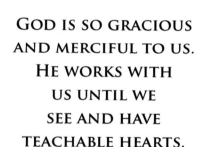

GOD IS SO GRACIOUS AND MERCIFUL TO US. HE WORKS WITH US UNTIL WE SEE AND HAVE TEACHABLE HEARTS.

In the fall of 2003, the Lord spoke to me and said, "Prepare to move."

A few days later, the Lord spoke to me again, but this time He said, "I want you to move."

I asked, "Where?"

He gave me a picture and I knew it was Caldwell. I knew this would trouble Milo, so I repeated what the Lord had said to him and let it go.

A few days went by and a friend of mine stopped on her way home to Washington State.

Her first words were, "Where are you moving?"

I answered with a question, "What makes you think we are moving?"

She answered, "Patt, you know that every time I come to see you, I first ask the Lord if He has anything He wants me to know. When I asked the Lord this time, I saw your house was packed with boxes like someone who is getting ready to move."

I then shared with her what the Lord had been saying to me.

When Milo came home, I told him what my friend had said. Four months later, we moved to a new house in the town the Lord had shown me.

I was sure I had lost most of my friends in one church. They decided I was the problem in the church. I asked the Lord what I had done to cause this response.

He said, "I have positioned you in the place where you will see and sense danger for this group. They did not like how you were standing in your position."

I asked Him if I had done something wrong.

He answered, "You are where I have placed you."

A few days later, I was standing in front of the mirror combing my hair and I said to the Lord, "I lost all my friends."

His response was, "I lost all My friends, too."

I knew He was talking about His disciples not standing with Him all the way from the Garden of Gethsemane to the Cross. He healed my heart with those words.

As I was praying and worshipping the Lord, I saw the world-wide Church trying to sail the sea of God in clipper ships. I was aware the people of God did not know how to catch the winds of His Spirit, causing them to be stationary.

"Lord, I pray that your Body would awaken to your winds and how to navigate on the sea of Your Spirit.

MAY WE LISTEN TO YOUR VOICE AND OBEY.

The Lord said, "I don't hold your failures against you. Go in My name and be a witness to My mercy and grace."

As far as the east is from the west, so far has he removed our transgressions from us. (Psalm 103:12 NIV)

"Go therefore and make disciples of all the nations, baptizing them in the name of the Father and of the Son and of the Holy Spirit, teaching them to observe all things that I have commanded you; and lo, I am with you always, even to the end of the age." Amen. (Matthew 28:19-20 NKJV)

The Lord said, "'Know your days are in my hands. Do not become weary in well doing" (see Galatians 6:9-10).

The Lord said, "My timing is always right."

"Therefore judge nothing before the appointed time; wait till the Lord comes. He will bring to light what is hidden in darkness and will expose the motives of men's hearts. At that time each will receive his praise from God." (1 Corinthians 4:5 NIV)

I heard the Lord say, "You want to serve Me perfectly, but the natural man is unable to do so. It is by My Spirit you're able to serve Me with right motives and actions. I search each person's motives and choices."

"For the eyes of the Lord range throughout the earth to strengthen those whose hearts are fully committed to him." (2 Chronicles 16:9 NIV)

I prayed, "Teach us Lord to live by faith and not fall into works."

As I was worshiping the Lord I started singing these words:

WHAT AN ASSURANCE WHEN WE FAIL THE LORD OR WANDER OFF. HE IS ALWAYS SEEKING FOR THE LOST AND STRAYING.

"If My people who are called by My Name understood that I am Good.

They would find peace of mind, joy divine, and victory all the time.

They would walk in the power of Jesus;

They would speak in the Name of My Son.

Yes, they would know I AM Good; yes, they would know I AM God."

The Lord said, "There is no depth or crevice so isolated or so deep that I cannot reach, touch, and redeem My wandering sheep from destruction."

In the earlier years of ministry, I was under great stress. Knowing I would have a hard time quieting my soul before falling asleep, I asked, "Lord, would You please hold my hand."

I could immediately sense my hand in His, giving me peace and rest. I drifted off to sleep.

WHAT A COMPASSIONATE GOD WE SERVE!

During the night, I awoke and was startled

as there was someone holding my hand and it wasn't my husband.

I then heard the Lord say, "You asked Me to hold your hand."

Have a Teachable Heart

Do you see the Lord as your greenhouse? _____

How much time do you spend in His presence getting the nourishment and spiritual water you need for your spiritual life? _____

I know and believe that God never violates man's will, but I also know God has wonderful ways of working in us until we willingly follow His calling for our lives. Too often we think we know the will of God, but more often it proves to be our own thinking. God is so gracious and merciful to us. He works with us until we see and have teachable hearts.

Do you have a teachable heart? _____

There is no peace without Him. If you need peace run to Father God and tell Him your need.

Do you know the peace that surpasses understanding?

Are you coming to His presence with a heart wanting to know and commune with Him? _____

> *"For the eyes of the Lord range throughout the earth to strengthen those whose hearts are fully committed to him."* (2 Chronicles 16:9 NIV)

Pray: *Lord, I humble myself before You, I truly seek Your face. I desire to have a teachable heart so You can use me to help heal this land. Thank You for Your mercy and forgiveness when I seek to do my will instead of Yours. I love You, Lord, and want to do what pleases You. Please teach me to be more and more like You.*

CHAPTER 6
THE FATHER'S HEART

These are some of Father God's replies to my request of what was on His heart. I prayed as He requested.

♥ Pray against, "The abruptness of my people. They make hasty abrupt decisions without thinking it through or consulting Me."

> *Forgive us, Father and teach us to bring*
> *everything to You until Your peace comes*
> *so we will not trust our own thinking.*

♥ He said, "The people of My Church enter the Tabernacle of My presence, but fail to wash at the laver. They just proceed into the Holy Place. They try to worship Me at the Golden Altar of incense. As a result, they have difficulty entering into My rest, peace, and intimate presence, so the fire within them goes out. Many churches do not allow time prior to praise and worship and for My people to wash away anything that comes from the world or has contaminated them. If they would take the time, they would more readily enter into the true spiritual worship that I desire. They would also leave the house of the Lord refreshed."

> *"I must be respected as holy by those who come near me; before all the people I must be given honor."* (Leviticus 10:3 NCV)

> *"Yet a time is coming and has now come when the true worshipers will worship the Father in spirit and truth, for they are the kind of worshipers the Father seeks. 24 God is spirit and his worshipers must worship in spirit and in truth."* (John 4:23-24 NIV)

Lord, let Your true worshipers come forth.

♥ "If My people would always stay submerged in My Word and Spirit, they would always be aware of My presence," He told me. "They would have great victory. However, too many lean to their own reasoning and follow it. Don't build your life on your decisions or experiences; instead, trust My Word and Holy Spirit to guide you."

Trust in the Lord with all your heart and lean not on your own understanding; in all your ways acknowledge him, and he will make your paths straight. Do not be wise in your own eyes; fear the Lord and shun evil. This will bring health to your body and nourishment to your bones. (Proverbs 3:5-8 NIV)

I prayed this scripture would become alive in the hearts of God's people.

♥ "I desire for My people to come to Me before they go to another for help," He said almost sadly. "All the help they need comes from Me."

Blessed is the man who walks not in the counsel of the ungodly, nor stands in the path of sinners, nor sits in the seat of the scornful; But his delight is in the law of the Lord, and in His law he meditates day and night. (Psalm 1:1-2 NKJV)

Lord, cause Your people to seek Your counsel instead of men's.

♥ "Pray that the lack of love for My Word would be defeated and they would seek Me daily by studying to show themselves approved by Me."

> *Teach me Your way, O Lord; I will walk in Your truth; Unite my heart to fear Your name. I will praise You, O Lord my God, with all my heart, And I will glorify Your name forevermore.* (Psalm 86:11-12 NKJV)

I prayed that His children would praise Him with all their hearts, love Him with their whole hearts, and love His Word and His presence.

♥ "Pray that My people would learn to worship Me in Spirit and Truth," He said.

> *God is Spirit, and those who worship Him must worship in spirit and truth."* (John 4:24 NKJV)

I prayed as the Lord had asked.

♥ He told me, "Pray for the President of the U.S. and that this country would remember its foundation and once again put their trust in Me."

Therefore, I exhort first of all that supplications, prayers, intercessions, and giving of thanks be made for all men, for kings and all who are in authority, that we may lead a quiet and peaceable life in all godliness and reverence. For this is good and acceptable in the sight of God our Savior, who desires all men to be saved and to come to the knowledge of the truth. (1 Timothy 2:1-5 NKJV)

I prayed as the Lord requested.

♥ "Pray for My people who copy My ways, but do not allow Me to change them," He asked of me.

This made me think of, "Remember this! In the last days there will be [people who] act as if they serve God but will not have his power" (2 Timothy 3:1, 5 NCV).

I continually pray for those who have an appearance of being Christ-like, but lack fruit.

♥ "Oh, that My people would truly hunger and thirst for My Word," God said passionately.

> *Blessed are those who hunger and thirst for righteousness, for they will be filled.* (Matthew 5:6 NIV)

Blessed is the man who does not walk in the counsel of the wicked or stand in the way of sinners or sit in the seat of mockers. But his delight is in the law of the Lord, and on his law he meditates day and night. (Psalm 1:1-2 NIV)

I prayed that we would all hunger and thirst for His righteousness and delight in His laws and His ways.

♥ God said, "I desire a face to face relationship with everyone who says they belong to Me. If they would do this, they will know My ways and find intimacy with Me."

Who may ascend the hill of the Lord? Who may stand in his holy place? He who has clean hands and a pure heart, who does not lift up his soul to an idol or swear by what is false. He will receive blessing from the Lord and vindication from God his Savior. (Psalm 24:3-5 NIV)

Open the eyes of our hearts, Lord, to see Your love and Your desire for a relationship with us as a loving father desires a relationship with his children.

♥ "I desire for My people to come and take the position in My Body that I have assigned them," God said referring to 1 Peter 2:5.

> "...you also, like living stones, are being built into a spiritual house to be a holy priest-hood, offering spiritual sacrifices accept-able to God through Jesus Christ." (NIV)

As we seek His face and His will for our lives, I pray we would all put action to our faith and begin to actively fill our positions in the Body of Christ.

♥ "I want My people to come to My table for the right reasons—not just to fellowship with others. I desire true intimacy so My imparted truths and revelation will be heard and obeyed," He told me.

> "Come, all you who are thirsty, come to the waters; and you who have no money, come, buy and eat! Come, buy wine and milk without money and without cost. Why spend money on what is not bread, and your labor on what does not satisfy? Listen, listen to me, and eat what is good, and your soul will delight in the richest of fare." (Isaiah 55:1-2 NIV)

It broke my heart to hear Father God lamenting over His children's selfish ways. I prayed we all would show our love for Him by how we respect His house and treat it with reverence.

♥ "Pray that My people would quit just poking at the enemy of their souls. They seldom if ever take their stance of authority in Me," He said.

> *Whoever believes and is baptized will be saved, but whoever does not believe will be condemned. And these signs will accompany those who believe: In my name they will drive out demons; they will speak in new tongues; they will pick up snakes with their hands; and when they drink deadly poison, it will not hurt them at all; they will place their hands on sick people, and they will get well."* (Mark 16:16-18 NIV)

> *Put on the full armor of God so that you can take your stand against the devil's schemes. For our struggle is not against flesh and blood, but against the rulers, against the authorities, against the powers of this dark world and against the spiritual forces of evil in the heavenly realms. Therefore, put on*

*the full armor of God, so that when the day
of evil comes, you may be able to stand your
ground, and after you have done everything,
to stand.* (Ephesians 6:11-13 NIV)

Power and authority belongs to those who believe.
We need to seriously ask ourselves, am I a believer? If
I am, why am I not living in my God-given authority and
doing what He has equipped us to do?

♥ The Lord said, "I desire that the blinders on the eyes
of My people would be removed."

*His divine power has given us everything
we need for life and godliness through our
knowledge of him who called us by his own
glory and goodness. Through these he has
given us his very great and precious promises, so that through them you may par-
ticipate in the divine nature and escape
the corruption in the world caused by evil
desires. For this very reason, make every
effort to add to your faith goodness; and to
goodness, knowledge; and to knowledge,
self-control; and to self-control, perseverance; and to perseverance, godliness; and
to godliness, brotherly kindness; and to*

brotherly kindness, love. For if you possess these qualities in increasing measure, they will keep you from being ineffective and unproductive in your knowledge of our Lord Jesus Christ. But if anyone does not have them, he is nearsighted and blind, and has forgotten that he has been cleansed from his past sins. (2 Peter 1:3-9)

Lord, cause us to see how You have equipped each of us to be Your representatives to this hurting world.

♥ He said, "Pray for My people who live like the world and just nibble on the things of God."

So I say, live by the Spirit, and you will not gratify the desires of the sinful nature. For the sinful nature desires what is contrary to the Spirit, and the Spirit what is contrary to the sinful nature. They are against each other, so that you do not do what you want. But if you are led by the Spirit, you are not under law. (Galatians 5:16-18 NIV)

Father, I asked that great hunger would arise within those who just nibble on spiritual things. May there truly be turnabout in the hearts of Your children who are just drifting and not moving forward in their faith.

♥ He said, "Pray for My people to understand that beauty is not in one's appearance but in one's heart."

> *"The Lord does not look at the things man looks at. Man looks at the outward appearance, but the Lord looks at the heart."* (1 Samuel 16:7 NIV)

Lord, let all of us truly know that true beauty comes from our hearts.

♥ "I gave My very best and yet many people still reject Me and think I don't care. They accuse Me of being unjust and unloving. Each man chooses what he wants to believe."

"Lord, I pray for everyone who sees You as not being just, fair or loving. I know our wrong perceptions have caused us to see You incorrectly. May our eyes be opened and our ears hear Your truth? Bring repentance to our hearts.

> *The Lord has appeared of old to me, saying:*
> *"Yes, I have loved you with an everlasting*

love; Therefore, with lovingkindness I have drawn you. (Jeremiah 31:3 NKJV)

♥ He said, "Pray for My people to see their complacency."

I prayed, *"Forgive us Lord for being content with where we are. Cause us to daily seek You and Your will for our day."*

> *We want each of you to show this same dili-gence to the very end, in order to make your hope sure. We do not want you to become lazy, but to imitate those who through faith and patience inherit what has been prom-ised.* (Hebrews 6:11-12 NIV)

♥ He instructed me, "Pray for those who have been blinded by what man says is truth."

I prayed, *"Forgive us for not holding to the truth of Your Word or believing it. Forgive us for submitting to the ways and thoughts of the world. I ask that everyone blinded by humanism will see the Truth and repent."*

> *Satan, who is the god of this world, has blinded the minds of those who don't believe. They are unable to see the glorious light of*

the Good News. They don't understand this message about the glory of Christ, who is the exact likeness of God. (2 Corinthians 4:4 NLT)

♥ He told me, "I desire for My people to come to faith and reject working to please Me. Faith must precede works."

"So then faith comes by hearing, and hearing by the word of God." (Romans 10:17 NKJV)

I diligently prayed, *"May we seek to hear His Word, listen to hear His voice, and then put action to our ever-increasing faith."*

♥ He asked me to, "Pray for those who will be facing the horrors to come."

So, I prayed, *"Lord, let our hearts respond to You now, so when trouble comes we will know and see You as our protector and provider."*

Men will faint from terror, apprehensive of what is coming on the world, for the heavenly bodies will be shaken. At that time they will see the Son of Man coming in a cloud with power and great glory. When these

*things begin to take place, stand up and lift
up your heads, because your redemption is
drawing near." (Luke 21:26-28 NIV)*

*For rulers hold no terror for those who do
right, but for those who do wrong. (Romans
13:3-4 NIV)*

Do you want to be free from fear of the one who
has all authority?
Then do what is right and He will commend you.

Praying the Father's Heart

*His divine power has given us everything
we need for life and godliness through our
knowledge of him who called us by his own
glory and goodness. Through these he has
given us his very great and precious promises, so that through them you may par-
ticipate in the divine nature and escape
the corruption in the world caused by evil
desires. For this very reason, make every
effort to add to your faith goodness; and to
goodness, knowledge; and to knowledge,
self-control; and to self-control, perseverance; and to perseverance, godliness; and*

to godliness, brotherly kindness; and to brotherly kindness, love. For if you possess these qualities in increasing measure, they will keep you from being ineffective and unproductive in your knowledge of our Lord Jesus Christ. But if anyone does not have them, he is nearsighted and blind, and has forgotten that he has been cleansed from his past sins. (2 Peter 1:3-9)

As I sought the Father's heart, I saw the Lion of Judah, so I prayed, *"Father, I asked that Your qualities would arise within every believer. Cause us to submit to Your work in us and to stand in Your delegated authority until the boldness to win the lost and to overcome the enemy comes forth."*

It's time for you to pray as He has requested. Go back over each of these requests of the Lord and pray as His Spirit directs you. Then seek other ways you can become a productive and effective part of the Body of Christ.

CHAPTER 7

LEARNING TO HEAR GOD

Learning is easy for many and difficult for others. Although, I am a normally a good learner, I did not always learn what the Lord was telling me until much later. With time and diligence, I find it much easier now. With diligence you can also learn to be a good learner.

As I was falling asleep, I saw myself ringing an old crank wall phone.

Upon awaking I remembered it and asked the Lord, "What are You saying?"

I heard, "You are using an old method to contact Me."

This made me realize I hadn't been praying in the Spirit regularly. However, I have learned it is important to pray in the Spirit daily.

While at one church there was an individual who was not very happy with me. I had a dream that I picked up a board and slammed it into his midriff.

Upon awakening, I prayed, "O Lord, please don't let me do that."

I should have prayed, "Lord, what is in me that would make me do that?" But I didn't.

One day, I made a comment in his presence about his not liking a particular song. As soon as I did, I remembered the dream. I knew I had just hit him in his soul realm. I asked God to forgive me and show me how to be wiser with my comments. I was full of remorse, but I had lost an opportunity to build a better relationship simply because I did not understand what the Lord was really warning me about.

WRONG CHOICES BRING WRONG ACTIONS.

There is now no condemnation for those who are in you. (Romans 8:1 NIV)

I dreamed Jonelle, our son's wife wanted me to meet their two sons. [They had no children.] The oldest was about two years old and was dressed in an outfit just like the one our son had at age two. The boy had dark hair like his mother. They had named him, Joshua. The second son was blonde, like Michael at one year. They had named him Andrew. Upon awaking, I wondered how they could have had two children without us knowing about it.

When they came to visit, I told Jonelle about the dream.

She responded, "I had a dream, too, where we had two boys and their names were Joshua and Andrew." I found that very interesting.

A few years later, on their annual summer visit they revealed they were not successful in conceiving and were going to have fertility treatment. The result was two miscarriages. I wondered if the two miscarriages were Joshua and Andrew. Only eternity will tell.

Before I formed you in the womb I knew you.
(Jeremiah 1:5 NIV)

Michael and Jonelle always leave very early on the day they return home. We got up with them to say our goodbyes. After they left, I went back to bed only to dream Jonelle lifted her shirt to show me she was pregnant. I could see she was about six or seven months pregnant. [End of dream.]

With no success getting pregnant, they decided to adopt. They made their application and waited. Finally, the day came when they were informed a baby girl was available for adoption. However, they were later disappointed as certain legal circumstances concerning the birth mother would not allow them to adopt the baby. They were devastated.

It took a long time before they even considered trying adoption again. After their emotions were semi-healed, they put in another application with a different agency. They waited and waited and finally a phone call came. They were told their baby girl had just been born and they needed to come get her. What a joyous phone call we received. Their baby girl has been a great delight to her parents and us.

When their little girl was about two and a half, I said to the Lord, "It's time to see the fulfillment of the dream about them having their own child."

The following week our son called to tell us, "We are pregnant."

About a week later, they called to tell us they would be having a son. When they came for their annual summer visit, Jonelle looked about seven months pregnant—just like in the dream. Their son was born two months later.

> GOD HAS A PURPOSE AND A TIME FOR ALL THINGS.

How wonderfully blessed they have been. God knows everything we will go through and it is always to bless us in the end. He uses our circumstances to cause us to grow and learn more about Him and His ways.

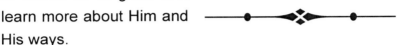

THANK YOU, LORD, FOR YOUR GOODNESS. YOUR TIMING IS PERFECT.

We know that all that happens to us is working for our good if we love God and are fitting into his plans (Romans 8:28 TLB)

While between churches, we visited a certain church. During that time, I basically had the same dream twice. In the first dream, I was attacked by a couple of men dressed in black and they raped me. Before we left that church, there were ones who attempted to slander, defame, and malign my character so I would not be used of God. I did better at dealing with this than I had in previous years.

A few years after this, I had another dream concerning the same issue. A huge black man with black clothing came into my bedroom and tried to rape me. I tried to get away by kicking him in his private area.

I failed in that attempt, so I started screaming to my sister in the next room, "Call 911, call 911."

The more I yelled 911, the more the man fell into a deep sleep and lost his hold on me. Finally, a string of white pearls fell out of the man's hand.

Black in this dream had nothing to do with race. It simply denoted being full of sin or evil. I knew 911 meant I was calling on Jesus, the only one who could save and deliver me. However, the string of pearls stumped me.

A few months after this dream, it dawned on me the pearls represented the valuable things the enemy had robbed from me. Jesus tells the parable of the pearl of great price in Matthew 13:45-46. The Lord and His truth are the greatest pearls of my life. The pearls falling from the man's hand told me the thief returned what he'd stolen.

The thief…must pay back seven times what he stole. (Proverbs 6:31 NLT)

"Because he loves me," says the Lord, "I will rescue him; I will protect him, for he acknowledges my name. He will call upon me, and I will answer him; I will be with him in trouble, I

HOW GREAT ARE THE LOVE, PROTECTION, PROVISION, AND REDEMPTION OF THE LORD!

*will deliver him and honor him. With long
life will I satisfy him and show him my salvation."* (Psalm 91:14-16 NIV)

I had a dream that the District Supervisor of the church
sent Milo and me to an isolated town in Wyoming. When
we arrived, I started walking around to look at the scenery.
I met a woman who said something about it being isolated
and lonely in that place. I could feel her hurt way down
deep inside myself. I just answered her by saying something about the scenery's beauty.

Upon awakening, I realized the Lord was showing me
that way down deep inside I believed He had sent me to a
place in my life that was lonely and isolated from healthy
Christians. I repented of that false belief for I knew He
had a purpose and a plan for wherever He would send
us. The Lord also ministered to me from His Word.

*But now thus says the Lord, he who created
you, O Jacob, he who formed you, O Israel:
Fear not, for I have redeemed you; I have
called you by name, you are mine. When
you pass through the waters, I will be with
you; and through the rivers, they shall not
overwhelm you; when you walk through fire*

you shall not be burned, and the flame shall not consume you. For I am the Lord your God, the Holy One of Israel, your Savior. (Isaiah 43:1-3 ESV)

In early 1980, I dreamed that I was going to visit my friend at her place of work. I knew there were slack times when she would be available to talk with me. However, when I arrived she was extremely busy, so I took a seat waiting for her free time.

> GOD'S WORD IS A SOURCE OF COMFORT NO MATTER WHAT STORM WE ARE GOING THROUGH.

The phone rang and when my friend answered it, she said, "Patt, this phone call is for you."

I was puzzled since no one knew I would be at my friend's office.

When I took the phone, a woman said, "My name is Sandy Trinity. I am calling to see how you are doing. I know you do not know me, but I know you." [I do not know any one by that name].

I said, "I am fine considering all the gossip that is going around about me."

Sandy responded, "I understand. I get the same kind of things from my family."

As I was talking to her, I somehow had the ability to see her. She had dark hair and seemed to be Jewish. [End of dream]

I pondered this dream for a while. Then I realized that the Lord had given me this dream as an encouragement. Sandra means "she knows" and "defender of man." Trinity is God in three forms—Father, Son, and Holy Spirit. Therefore, the Lord through the Holy Spirit was speaking to my troubled soul. The Lord knew there were some people who had maligned me just as His people had Him. What an amazing dream.

> *A student is not better than his teacher, and a servant is not better than his master. A student should be satisfied to become like his teacher; a servant should be satisfied to become like his master. If the head of the family is called Beelzebul, then the other members of the family will be called worse names!* (Matthew 10:24-25 NCV)

In the late 1970s, I dreamed I was sitting in a theater like building. I was observing the other people in my row.

They were all kneeling and facing the back of the building. There was great fear on their faces as they were very aware of the wrath of God that was about to come upon the earth. A young girl came in and sat down next to me. Then she joined all the others who were kneeling. She said she wanted me to protect her from the wrath of God.

Then the backdoor slammed shut with a loud reverberating sound. I somehow knew that the last one had been converted to Christ and the judgment of God was at hand.

The word "theater" comes from the Greek word *theaomai,* which translated means to gaze upon, to fully see, or to look at intently. I find this very interesting as I have had numerous dreams in theater like buildings. I now know that it represents an unveiling for people to fully see or intently look at something.

As you know, this dream has not happened as of yet, but it does reveal the terror that will be in the hearts of the lost. We need to be diligent to keep our lives pleasing to God and win the lost to Christ. We need to especially pray for those in our family and our friends who do not know Jesus as their personal Savior.. . Many people think just recognizing Jesus is God is sufficient, but they need to have a personal relationship received by faith.

Whoever believes in the Son has eternal life, but whoever rejects the Son will not see life, for God's wrath remains on him." (John 3:36 NIV)

He commanded us to preach to the people and to testify that he is the one whom God appointed as judge of the living and the dead. All the prophets testify about him that everyone who believes in him receives forgiveness of sins through his name." (Acts 10:42-43 NIV)

Within the last few months, I have dreamed there were a multitude of families seeking places to hide in the hills. I was shown a map of the area where each family was hiding. Soon there wasn't any room left for more hideouts.

They called to the mountains and the rocks, "Fall on us and hide us from the face of him who sits on the throne and from the wrath of the Lamb! For the great day of their wrath has come, and who can stand?" (Revelation 6:16-17 NIV)

Nothing in all creation is hidden from God's sight. Everything is uncovered and lay bare before the eyes of him to whom we must give account. (Hebrews 4:13 NIV)

There will be those who try to hide from God, but it is futile. We must be faithful to pray for the lost, and be alert and watch for the Lord's return.

Ask yourself if you are diligently praying for the lost? Now is the time we must pray for them. Ask God to give you a heart like His for the lost. Are you ready?

In recent years, I dreamed I was taking care of a boy and girl who were both around eight years old. We were standing on their front porch. As I looked around, I saw down through the trees to our left a pathway of fire forming. The fire continued to grow until it was a whirlwind that was twenty to thirty feet taller than the trees and forty to fifty feet wide. I could feel the forceful winds of the fire coming towards us. However, the fire was not consuming anything. I awoke when the fire reached the house where I was standing with the two children.

My heart was doing triple time as I asked the Lord what He was saying.

He said, "The fire is like the burning bush where I told Moses, 'This is holy ground.' It represents My holiness and its purifying qualities."

As I was looking at the fire and standing in the Lord's presence, I could see there was a black wooden stick stuck in my midriff. I asked the Lord the name on the stick.

He said, "Ego master." I realized a witchcraft curse had been placed on me to keep me from fulfilling my mission in Christ. I broke the power of the curse and any agreement I may have made with it in the name of Jesus. Then I did spiritual warfare against this Jezebel-spirited, strong man. The stick was removed and the Lord washed, purified, and filled the wound with His oil.

The next night, I dreamed that I was attending a certain church. All they allowed anyone to do was meet physical needs. There was no praying in the Spirit or manifestation of the gifts of the Spirit.

I awaken and instantly saw the fire of the whirlwind from the night before. I realized the Lord was answering the question of my heart, by showing me who the boy and girl represented. I immediately saw a couple and He said that

> OH, HOW GOD LOVES US! ALL TOO OFTEN WE DON'T EVEN REALIZE WE ARE SHUNNING HIS LOVE.

they are holding on to the old beliefs and teachings hindering their growth in the Holy Spirit. I prayed they will hear what the Lord wants them to hear.

How patient and kind He is to all of us. Many times, we resist Him and don't know we have. We need to ask the Lord if there is anything within us that is resisting Him now. We also need to consistently pray for those who are hindered or have closed the door to the power of the Holy Spirit in their lives.

In the late 1970s, a friend came to me very concerned that her husband, Wade would lose his job. I prayed with her asking the Lord to intervene on Wade's behalf. One night following that request, I awoke from a dream knowing it concerned Wade. I knew it was important, but I couldn't remember it.

I said to the Lord, "If I am really to remember this dream and share it with her, please let me have the dream again."

I went back to sleep and had the identical dream a second time, but this time when I awoke I remembered it. The dream was short and sweet. I saw Wade was being handed the keys to the city. This was fulfilled quickly, for within a few weeks Wade was made Chief of Police. In essence, he was given the keys to the city.

> HOW WONDROUSLY ENCOURAGING AND TIMELY IS THE LORD IN FULFILLING HIS PLAN FOR EACH INDIVIDUAL LIFE. ALL GLORY AND HONOR ARE DUE HIM.

I dreamed another individual and I had been given a bag of gold, but these bags were at the bottom of a water tank. We were told to dive in and get our bag of gold. I hesitated because it looked too shallow. Again, I was told to go get my bag of gold. Finally, I dived into the water. I easily went to the bottom of the tank and picked up my bag of gold plus some for others. However, I was then told I had to throw back all that did not belong to me. I did as I was instructed and the dream ended.

The water represented the Word and the Spirit of God. The gold represented God's divinity and holiness. In other words, He had words of knowledge and spiritual gifts concerning His divinity and holiness available to me.

However, I had to throw back what was not mine because God wants us to seek and find what He has for us individually. We are not to try to get anything for another person. It is each person's responsibility to seek for the spiritual gift(s) or words God desires to give them. I am not to try to get people to hear as I hear. I must let God talk to me and empower me, just as He will for those who seek Him. This is His desire for every believer.

If the Lord gives me something for another person, that is different than when they want me to hear God for them. Over the years, I have learned that when the Lord gives me something for another, He will also open the door for me to share it. Usually, the person will bring the subject up and I know I am to bring confirmation through what He has told me about their situation.

I am uneasy with anyone wanting me to hear from God for them, especially after that dream. So, I have to find a way of gently saying to them, "You need to seek the Lord until you hear Him speak to your heart. He wants to interact with you."

> I ALWAYS ENCOURAGE OTHERS THAT WHAT GOD HAS DONE FOR ME HE WILL DO FOR THOSE WHO DILIGENTLY SEEK HIM.

One night I had just finished reading Psalm 91, a book about that psalm by Peggy Joyce Ruth. I fell asleep and dreamed I was in a corral with this raged-filled horse. His eyes were bulging, and he was filled with hate and fire. He was running and kicking his hind legs up from side to side. The horse came at me, yet I had no fear. The horse suddenly grabbed the back of my neck with his jaws. He began to shake me from side to side. I was not afraid even though the horse was trying to destroy me.

Upon awakening, my only thought was, "I really do have Psalm 91 deep in my heart."

I also know Satan will try to destroy me, but he will not prevail. What security, peace, and rest come from truly putting the Lord first! Read Psalm 91:14-16 and embrace the amazing truth of God's love, protection, and provision.

Early in our ministry, I dreamed a man was getting ready to put on a wig. Before he put it on, he put on what looked like a swimming cap in order to cover all his hair. Then he pulled on the wig. He looked at me and wanted me to do the same. However, the moment I did, it started suffocating me, so I took it off.

As a young Christian, the Lord showed me my hair revealed the state of my relationship with Him. From time to time, I have had dreams with my hair in many states from dry and brittle, fried, short, over-permed, or real long. Most of the time, it was other people who were working on or cutting my hair, so it was unbecoming, ragged, and totally not me. How they fixed my hair was how they believed God saw me. Therefore, my understanding of this dream was others wanted me to have their type of false relationship with the Lord—one that covers up and then substitutes a false outward appearance rather than a true relationship with the Lord.

I want to be genuine before God and others. I would truly suffocate if I had to act, speak, or think like someone else. As God's people, we should always want the relationship with Him He desires. He always sees us through eyes of love.

God Speaks in Many Ways

"*My sheep hear My voice, and I know them, and they follow Me.*" (John 10:27 NKJV)

HOW LOVING, KIND, GRACIOUS, AND FORGIVING IS OUR GOD.

A common stumbling block in hearing and understanding the Lord is presumption [trusting our own thinking to be right]. I had a dream I thought was ludicrous. I was driving our little Ford Fiesta down Main Street. The next thing I knew, a big dog jumped right in front of my face into the car. I stopped and got out. I was horrified.

Trusting my own thinking, I hadn't even given a thought that this dream might be a warning. I presumed, and it led to deception and sin [not trusting God].

However, a few weeks later this dream was physically fulfilled. An Afghan hound jumped through the open window right in front of my eyes while I was driving on Main Street. I stopped and got out as fast as possible. I thought the dog was crazy. The dog was too big and too difficult for me to remove, so a man from the street came to my rescue. [It wasn't his dog.]

I hadn't asked the Lord for His wisdom concerning the dream, so I reaped the fruit of leaning to my own thinking. King David prayed. "Keep me from presumptuous sin" (Psalm 9:13 NKJV).

Praying about what we hear, see and/or receive until we have the peace of God will bring security and faith. The more we trust what He says and act on it the more our faith will grow. Faith in Him causes us to listen carefully

Quite often God speaks to me through dreams. However, He may speak to others in different ways. Over the years, I have learned there are some basic ways the Lord speaks.

- An inward conviction
- Scriptural confirmation—when a scripture jumps out at you
- Prophetic confirmation—--when God uses an anointed individual to say what you need to hear
- Godly counsel—Words of God's wisdom from godly counselors
- Circumstances—causing you to see and understand God's will for your situation.
- God's provision
- Dreams, visions
- Peace of God

All of these are ways that God has spoken to me, but I knew there had to be an absolute way to give me assurance and faith. Seven of the ways listed can be influenced by our own wants, desires, appetites, and thinking, or by other people's opinions, or Satan's influence or suggestions. Satan cannot counterfeit the peace of God that surpasses understanding.

Have you tuned your ears to hear the Spirit of God?
Have you heard Him speak, and then obeyed?
Have you let fear lead you to do nothing?
How can one be sure it is God speaking?

The Lord has given one absolute proof God is speaking—the Peace of God that passes understanding. Satan cannot counterfeit God's peace as he has no relationship with

> I WILL MAKE PEACE YOUR GOVERNOR AND RIGHTEOUSNESS YOUR RULER.
> (ISAIAH 60:17 NIV)

God. It is God's peace we need for every situation and word. Many have said, "I have peace" only to find out later, it was the world's peace, not God's.

The peace of God and righteousness are always joined. Our relationship with God must be up to date or God's peace will not rule us. Praying about what we hear, see, and/or receive until we have God's peace will bring security and faith. The more we trust what He says and act on it the more our faith will grow. Faith causes us to listen carefully.

When we were pastoring a certain church, there was a young woman—I'll call her Jane. The Lord had revealed to me Jane had a deep-seated bitterness in her heart. One day, Jane became very ill, so I went to visit her. While in conversation, an opportunity presented itself, so I could ask if there was someone in her past she had not forgiven.

She immediately replied, "Yes, I've tried numerous times and think I have peace, only for bitterness to raise its head again."

I counseled her, "You must ask God's forgiveness for holding a grudge. Then forgive the individual and declare, 'I forgive _____.' Be sure to forgive yourself for allowing bitterness a foothold. And lastly, you need to call the individual and make it right."

While talking to her, I shared that there is a peace the world and the flesh will give, but the peace of God is much deeper—totally restful and lasting. Peace that surpasses understanding means there is no natural reason to be peace-filled according to circumstances or one's thinking.

A few weeks later, Jane told me she had followed my advice, called the man, and he was surprised she had even been offended. He gladly forgave her. She said that she never knew there was a peace like she received by forgiving that man. She had finally experienced the peace of God that surpasses understanding.

*I am leaving you with a gift—peace of mind
and heart. And the peace I give is a gift the
world cannot give.* (John 14:27 NLT)

*You, Lord, give true peace to those who
depend on you, because they trust you.*
(Isaiah 26:3 NCV)

God intimately and fully knows you. (See Psalm 139:13- 14).

Too often we let our own thinking block out His voice. Do you believe the Lord desires to talk to you? If you do, choose to silence your flesh by submitting your mind, will, emotions, and thinking to Him. Then choose to hear His will and words above your own.

You may think you do not have any God given dreams and visions that will direct you as I have had. One must remember God deals with each of us differently. He made us different for His purpose and reasons. We are not all dreamers or seers, but too many of us are not hearers either. God talks to all believers. We just need to learn to listen.

Jesus told the churches in Revelation, "He who has an ear, let him hear what the Spirit says." Have you tuned your ears to hear the Spirit of God? As believers we will hear if we choose to listen.

What Hinders One from Hearing God

Incorrect God Concepts:
* God does not involve Himself with humanity anymore.
* God is not all powerful.
* One can only go to the Lord with big things or at certain times and places.
* God is always watching to see what I do wrong.
* God will always ask me to do what I don't want or like to do.
* God is limited by man's will.
* God doesn't know what man is thinking.
* God deals with everyone exactly the same.
* God requires the letter of the law.

Bitterness: *"Let all bitterness, wrath, anger, clamor, and evil speaking be put away from you, with all malice. And be kind to one another, tenderhearted, forgiving one another, even as God in Christ forgave you."* (Ephesians 4:31-32 NKJV)

Rejection: Believing others do not accept you.

"God decided in advance to adopt us into his own family by bringing us to himself through Jesus Christ. This is what he wanted to do, and it gave him great pleasure." (Ephesians 1:5-6 NLT)

Rebellion: Doing what you want regardless of God's will, governing authorities, or parents. *"Do not harden*

139

your hearts as in the rebellion, In the day of trial in the wilderness, Where your fathers tested Me, tried Me, And saw My works forty years. Therefore I was angry with that generation, And said, 'They always go astray in their heart, And they have not known My ways.' So I swore in My wrath, 'They shall not enter My rest.'" (Hebrews 3:8-11 NKJV)

Hearing Incorrectly: Having a different meaning for words used than the one speaking. Hearing incorrectly includes: 1) misunderstanding what they are saying, 2) not liking how words are used, 3) being disturbed by the way they speak, 4) feeling their mannerisms and presentation is in appropriate. Multiple times one individual told me she knew I was upset because of the look on my face. She would tell me what was said and I wasn't upset in any of her examples. It was just a wrong perception.

"Therefore take heed how you hear." (Luke 8:18 NKJV)

Being Presumptuous: Rash or hasty.

"'But the person who does anything presumptuously,… that person shall be completely cut off; his guilt shall be upon him.'" (Numbers 15:30-31 NKJV)

"The Lord knows how to deliver the godly out of temptations and to reserve the unjust under punishment for the day of judgment, and especially those who walk according to the flesh in the lust of uncleanness and

despise authority. They are presumptuous, self-willed."
(2 Peter 2:9-10 NKJV)

Failing to Die to Self Daily:

"If anyone desires to come after Me, let him deny himself, and take up his cross daily, and follow Me." (Luke 9:23 NKJV)

Hardness of Heart:

"Later He [Jesus] appeared to the eleven as they sat at the table; and He rebuked their unbelief and hardness of heart, because they did not believe those who had seen Him after He had risen." (Mark 16:14-15 NKJV)

Lack of Knowledge:

"My people are destroyed from lack of knowledge." (Hosea 4:6 NIV)

"The fear of the Lord is the beginning of knowledge, but fools despise wisdom and discipline." (Proverbs 1:7 NIV)

Carnal Nature:

"For the flesh lusts against the Spirit, and the Spirit against the flesh; and these are contrary to one another, so that you do not do the things that you wish. But if you are led by the Spirit, you are not under the law. Now the works of the flesh are evident, which are: adultery, fornication, uncleanness, lewdness, idolatry, sorcery, hatred,

contentions, jealousies, outbursts of wrath, selfish ambitions, dissensions, heresies, envy, murders, drunkenness,
revelries, and the like; of which I tell you beforehand, . .
. that those who practice such things will not inherit the
kingdom of God." (Galatians 5:17-21 NKJV)

Unteachable: [Not open to anything different than
what one already thinks.]

"For My thoughts are not your thoughts, nor are your
ways My ways," declares the Lord. "For as the heavens
are higher than the earth, so are My ways higher than
your ways, and My thoughts than your thoughts." (Isaiah
55:8-9 NASB)

"There is a way that seems right to a man, but in the
end it leads to death." (Proverbs 16:25 NIV)

Wrong Perceptions:

"This is why I speak to them in parables: 'Though
seeing, they do not see; though hearing, they do not
hear or understand. In them is fulfilled the prophecy of
Isaiah: '...you will be ever seeing but never perceiving.
For this people's heart has become calloused." (Matthew
13:13-15 NIV)

Undisciplined Emotions: Anger, being critical,
judging, and cursing.

Ungodly Soul Ties: One tied mentally, emotionally, physically, and spiritually in an ungodly way to another individual; such as ties to the occult, drugs, immorality, bitterness, etc.

Inattentiveness: Not listening or disciplining your mind to focus on God.

CONCLUSION:
NUGGETS OF WISDOM MINED FROM JAMES

I n closing, I want to leave you with wisdom nuggets. One of the most powerful ways for you to begin to hear from God is to dig deeply into His Word. For example, the Lord showed me some powerful truths as I "mined for nuggets" from the Book of James.

> *If you need wisdom, ask our generous God, and he will give it to you. He will not rebuke you for asking. But when you ask him, be sure that your faith is in God alone. Do not waver, for a person with divided loyalty is as unsettled as a wave of the sea that is blown and tossed by the wind. Such people should not expect to receive anything from*

the Lord. Their loyalty is divided between God and the world, and they are unstable in everything they do. (James 1:5-8 NLT)

Nuggets Found:

We are to ask for wisdom.
God freely gives wisdom.
We must ask believing (i.e. have faith).
Doubting results in not hearing God.

Therefore, submit to God. Resist the devil and he will flee from you. Draw near to God and He will draw near to you. Cleanse your hands, you sinners; and purify your hearts, you double-minded. Lament and mourn and weep! Let your laughter be turned to mourning and your joy to gloom. Humble yourselves in the sight of the Lord, and He will lift you up. (James 4:7-10 NKJV)

Nuggets Found:

Every nugget found is a command. Therefore, we must take a step towards God if we want His Presence.

"Submit yourself to God. . ." (Verse 7)

What does it mean to submit?

1. Asking God's forgiveness for any known sin.
2. Choosing God's will above your own.
3. Asking God to reveal anything that would hinder your communication with Him.
4. Breaking any judgments against self and others.
5. Removing any curse that comes with the judgments from others or yourself (1 Peter 3:16).
6. Dealing with anything else God reveals.
7. Submitting the members of your body to be instruments of righteousness (See Romans 6:13). Some of your members are your mind, will, and emotions, attitudes, desires, appetites, mindsets, and perceptions.
8. Taking the time to sing and worship until His presence comes.
9. Listening for the Lord's voice.
10. Choosing to hear what Holy Spirit is saying!

"Resist the devil and he will flee from you" (verse 7).

And these signs will accompany those who believe: In my name they will drive out demons. (Mark 16:17 NIV)

1. Bind Satan, any strong man, and his minions in Jesus' name.
2. Silence all demonic activity and render them unable to interfere with your communication with God in Jesus' name.
3. Satan has to flee, if you resist him in Jesus' name.

"Draw near to God" (James 4:8).

We must take a step towards God if we want God's Presence.

Put on the whole armor of God (Ephesians 6:11-18).

*Belt of Truth:
   We are told in John 1 Jesus is the Word and the Word is Truth.
*Breastplate of Righteousness:
   Righteousness is right standing with God (1 Corinthians 1:30).
*Gospel of Peace:
   Not the world's peace but God's (Ephesians 2:14).
*Shield of Faith: Deal with double mindedness (Romans 10:16-17).
   One must believe the Word of God. Faith and fear cannot dwell together, one or the other will rule (James 1:5).
   Doubt interferes with hearing God.

*Helmet of Salvation: Salvation is to change and protect one's thinking.

Salvation is knowing you are in right relationship with God and living according to His standards.

The one who is saved will declare, "I am a child of God, loved, forgiven, accepted, and seated in heavenly places with Him."

*Praying in the Spirit and in one's native language.

Remember, dialogue with God is a two-way conversation!

"He will draw near you!" (Verse 8)

1. The Lord is always present.
2. Wait quietly before Him.
3. Make your request known (Philippians 4:6-7).
4. Commune with the Lord. However, just talking and not listening is a monologue. Wait for His answers as they give life and light.

"Lament, weep, mourn, and repent!" (James 4:9).

1. Have godly sorrow.
2. See your sin as God sees it.
3. Then confess it and accept His forgiveness.
4. Let the joy and peace of God rule your heart and mind.

5. Give thanks.
6. Obey whatever He says to you.
7. Obedience brings rest and blessing.

I pray that through this book the Lord has blessed, encouraged, and challenged you to hear what He is saying to you and how to pray for others. As the Lord commanded Moses to bless the Israelites, so I will bless you.

> *"The Lord bless you and keep you; The Lord make His face shine upon you, and be gracious to you; The Lord lift up His countenance upon you, and give you peace."* (Numbers 6:24-26 NKJV)

About the Author

Patricia (Patt) Salmeier and her husband Milo have been in the ministry since 1970. They have pastored churches in Idaho, Oregon, and Washington. The first ten years were served in a traditional denominational church setting. The last thirty-six years, they have been pioneering independent Spirit-filled churches. Patt has been involved in teaching, preaching, and leading worship. Patt and Milo have three children and six grandchildren. They currently live in Caldwell, Idaho.

Any comments or questions?
Patt may be contacted at:

jewelsfromheavenps@gmail.com

END NOTES

1   There's Something about that Name" Gloria Gaither | William J. Gaither © 1970 William J. Gaither, Inc. (Admin. by Gaither Copyright Management

2   How Great is Your Goodness Ed Kerr ©1993 Integrity's Hosanna! Music (Admin. by Capitol CMG Publishing (Integrity Music [DC Cook])).)

3   There's a River of Life Betty Carr Pulkington / Lee Casebolt © 1971, 1975 Celebration

4   Safe Am I Mildred Dillon   1912

CPSIA information can be obtained
at www.ICGtesting.com
Printed in the USA
FFOW03n1851040118
44289892-43878FF